FEB 1 9 2013

D0741850

ALSO BY CHRISTOPHER WEST

*The Ecstasy of Saint Teresa*, Santa Maria della Vittoria; Rome, Italy
(Photoservice Electa/Getty Images)

# FILL
# THESE
# HEARTS

### GOD, SEX, AND THE
### UNIVERSAL LONGING

*Christopher West*

IMAGE
New York

Library of Congress Cataloging-in-Publication Data is available upon
request.

ISBN   978-0-307-98713-6
eISBN 978-0-307-98714-3

Printed in the United States of America

Book design by Jaclyn Reyes
Jacket design by Henning Communications, Inc.
Jacket photography © David McLeod Lewis

10 9 8 7 6 5 4 3 2 1

First Edition

*In gratitude to Jason,
Mark, Dave, and Mike*

# CONTENTS

# WHAT THIS BOOK IS ABOUT

## DESIRE

*This book is about desire.* Not trivial desires. Not superficial wants. This book is about the atomic energy of our souls—that universal "ache" and longing we feel as human beings for *something*. Where does that hungry void in us come from? Why do we have it? What are we supposed to *do* with it? More important, is there anything that can fill it? Does that "something" we're looking for even exist, and is there any hope of finding it? In short, is there hope that we can satisfy our deepest desire for happiness, for lasting fulfillment?

One can hardly speak of human *desire,* of course, without speaking about the power and pull of sexual desire. The sexual relationship holds out a seemingly irresistible promise of happiness. For many, sexual love seems to offer the one chance of filling that void inside with something close to satisfaction. What role does sexuality play in our search for happiness? We live in a culture sated with sex, but we remain starved for love. Why is that? How can we integrate spirituality and sexuality so as to learn how to love in and through our bodies as men and women made in God's image?

## DESIGN

*This book is about God's loving design for our happiness as men and women.* If God is the author of our humanity, he is also the author of human desire, including sexual desire. Why did he make us as sexual beings? Why did he make sex so pleasurable, so alluring and attractive? Was it only to dangle a carrot in front of our noses and then forbid us the satisfaction of eating it?

What does the very design of our bodies as male and female tell us about God's plan for our lives? Is the purpose of sex just to continue the species? Or is there something deeper, something grander, something beyond the merely physical at work here? Is there a larger, mysterious interplay between sex and the very meaning of existence? Might the whole reality of sex in the divine design be a foreshadowing of an eternal, heavenly bliss?

## DESTINY

*This is a book about our eternal destiny.* We are created for bliss, for ecstasy, and our hearts know it. According to the Christian faith, the ecstasy we yearn for at the deepest level of our being is precisely what God wants to give us—eternally. *That's* what makes the Gospel "good news." But a destiny of bliss is not simply a given.

The Latin *destinare* is an archer's term that means "to aim at." Desire has a trajectory. Wherever we aim it, that's where we will ultimately arrive. That's the tremendous gift and weighty responsibility of freedom. How do we distinguish authentic freedom from its counterfeits? How do we distinguish authentic love from its counterfeits? How do we place our freedom at the service of authentic love so as to arrive at our God-given destiny of heavenly bliss? As we will discover, this is what sexual morality, properly understood, is all about: learning how to aim our desire *for* heaven *toward* heaven.

## A DIALOGUE BETWEEN SACRED AND SECULAR

I am a student of both theology and pop culture. Although these two realms are sometimes far apart, I enjoy looking for God as much in a Hollywood movie or a pop song as I do in a theological tome. One has to be discerning when it comes to secular art (and theological tomes, I might add), but I subscribe to what Brother Lawrence taught about seeking God everywhere.

Since my last book (*At the Heart of the Gospel*) took a more formal theological approach, I felt it was time to take the conversation in a more casual direction. That's not to say we won't explore some profound mysteries in this book. We will. But my goal is to break them open in a kind of dialogue between sacred and secular sources.

For a few years now I've been working with a team of seasoned artists and musicians developing a live event that incorporates popular music, movie clips, YouTube videos, and other artistic works into a contemporary exposition of the Gospel. Typically presented in theaters rather than in churches, it's an attempt to step out "into the main streets," as Jesus said, "and invite everyone to the wedding feast" (Matt. 22:9). This book is named after that live event and takes the same approach in written form.

Art is the language of the heart. Sometimes a song lyric, a melody, or a movie scene can illuminate truths in a way that academic theology can't. And that is why even *secular* art can become the occasion of a *sacred* experience. As John Paul II wrote, "Even beyond its typically religious expressions, true art has a close affinity with the world of faith, so that, even in situations where culture and the Church are far apart, art remains a kind of bridge to religious experience."[1] This book, with its many references to the songs and movies of the culture, seeks to cross that bridge.

Of course, sacred sources establish the basis of the conversation. I draw primarily from the wisdom of Scripture, the writings of Christian saints throughout the ages, and from the vision of human love in the divine plan unfolded by the late John Paul II.

His magnificent *Theology of the Body,* as well as his pre-papal book *Love and Responsibility,* have offered Christians across denominational lines a bold, compelling, biblical response to the sexual revolution and have been the inspiration of my life's work.

In short, the simple and, at the same time, lofty goal of this book is to help us aim our *desire* according to God's *design* so we can safely arrive at our eternal *destiny*: bliss and ecstasy in union with God and one another forever. Desire, design, destiny: perhaps we could call it living our lives in 3D. Put even more succinctly, this book is a prayer, a cry welling up from that deep void in our being, for God to *fill these hearts.* I hope it blesses you on your journey.

# PART I

# DESIRE

*Desire:* an expressly felt yearning for something that promises to fill a void; a longing for that which promises satisfaction in its attainment. From the Latin *desiderare*: to long for, wish for, hope for, expect. The original sense may mean "to look to the stars" or "to await what the stars may bring" (from the phrase *de sidere*: "from the stars").

# CHAPTER I

# THE UNIVERSAL LONGING

*Everybody's got a hungry heart.*

—BRUCE SPRINGSTEEN[1]

In 1977 NASA launched *Voyager 1* and *Voyager 2* to explore the galaxy. A golden record called *The Sounds of Earth* was affixed to each of the twin spacecrafts—a message from earth to anyone out there in the universe who might be listening. It contained both music and the sound of a human heartbeat.

Annie Druyan served as the creative director of NASA's famous Voyager Interstellar Message (VIM) Project. Along with Carl Sagan and a few others, she was entrusted with the task of coming up with earth's message to the rest of the universe. Reflecting on the experience in a 2009 interview, she recalled,

The first thing I found myself thinking of was a piece by Beethoven from Opus 130, something called the Cavatina Movement . . . When I [first] heard this piece of music . . . I thought . . . Beethoven, how can I ever repay you? What can I ever do for you that would be commensurate with what you've just given me? And so, as soon as Carl said, "Well, we have this message, and it's going to last a thousand million years," I thought of . . . this great, beautiful, sad piece of music, on which Beethoven had written in the margin . . . the word *sehnsucht*, which is German for "longing." Part of what we wanted to capture in the Voyager message was this great longing we feel.[2]

A song of human longing launched into space . . . It's all the more poignant based on the Latin root of the word "desire" (*de sidere* — "from the stars"). It's as if NASA's scientists were saying to the rest of the universe: "This is who and what we are as human beings: creatures of longing." And hidden in that basic "introduction to who we are" seems a question for extraterrestrials, almost a test to see if we can relate to them: *Do you feel this too? Are we the only ones? Are we crazy?*

Perhaps even more we wanted to say to any other intelligent life out there, "*If you feel this longing, this ache for something too, what have you done with it? Have you discovered anything that can fill it or cure it?*" As Annie Druyan relates, "We were hoping that, you know, maybe things like passion and longing . . . are not just limited to our narrow experience but might be something . . . felt on other worlds."

And how best to communicate that longing we feel? Music. "We thought that the vibrations of the music would speak for us in ways that the machine itself and maybe the pictures and the other things that we had to offer wouldn't," explained Druyan.

## LONGING FOR THE TRUE, THE GOOD, AND THE BEAUTIFUL

What is it about music that can stir such emotion, tap into such profound movements and yearnings of the soul? I remember the first time I felt it. I was maybe eight years old, and Bruce Springsteen's anthem "Born to Run" came on the radio. At the end of the song as "the Boss" opened his rib cage and gave free rein to some kind of cosmic cry of his heart, something broke open inside me. I didn't even know what he was singing about, but lying in my bed with my head near the radio, it was as if a crack to the universe opened on my bedroom ceiling and something "ginormous" rumbled through my soul.

The music of Bruce Springsteen and U2 takes up a large section in the sound track of my life. So it was a special treat for me when Springsteen inducted U2 into the Rock and Roll Hall of Fame in 2005. That night the Boss put his finger on what I first felt lying in bed almost thirty years earlier: "A great rock band," he said, "searches for the same kind of combustible force that fueled the expansion of the universe after the big bang. They want

the earth to shake and spit fire, they want the sky to split apart
and for God to pour out." Then he paused and said a bit sheepishly, "It's embarrassing to want so much and expect so much
from music, except, sometimes it happens."[3]

Yes. Sometimes it happens. Sometimes we hear a certain
song or piece of music and it awakens something inexplicable at
our core . . . an ache, a burning, a throbbing, a yearning . . . Beneath our rather surface-y contentment with the workaday world,
beneath our desire to earn money and live until Friday, there's a
much deeper desire, isn't there? We've all felt it. Indeed, that collective cry that arises from the depths of our humanity for something to fill these hearts is what makes us human. *Desire* is part of
our *design,* and if we follow it through to its furthest reaches we
seem to intuit that it will lead us to our *destiny.*

That hunger, that nostalgia, that longing can be awakened
not only by a favorite song, but also by a favorite movie or poem,
or through an encounter with the beauty of creation (type "double rainbow" into YouTube for a dramatic example of the latter).
Sometimes it comes late at night when everything's quiet, we can't
sleep, and we're all alone with the rhythm of our own breathing
and heartbeat. In those moments, if we're brave enough to feel it,
we sense the desperation of our own poverty, our own need. We're
made for something *more.* And that "something more" is missing.
It eludes us. But whatever "it" is, *we want it.* And it hurts.

The Greek philosopher Plato called that interior yearning
*eros.* Eros was the Greek god of love and was identified by the Ro-

mans with Cupid. Cupid comes from the Latin word *cupere*, "to desire." Cupid, of course, conjures up the image of the winged boy with his bow and arrow. The human yearning we're exploring in this book can certainly be experienced as a kind of piercing arrow that wounds the heart, so to speak, making it "bleed" in a desperate search for satisfaction and fulfillment. But eros shouldn't be limited merely to romantic love or sexual desire. While eros certainly has sexual connotations that we shouldn't (and in this book won't) neglect, the meaning of eros is broader than that. Plato described eros as our longing for all that is true, good, and beautiful.[4] Sad thing is, most of us don't know where to direct that fire inside, so we end up getting burned and burning others. When that happens, the temptation can be to blame the "ache" itself, and to want to squelch it somehow, to snuff it out.

"Yet there is no escape from the burning desire within us for the true, the good, the beautiful," writes Dominican father and playwright Peter John Cameron. "Each of us lives with the unextinguishable expectation that life is supposed to make sense and satisfy us deeply. Even the most jaded atheist feels cheated if he doesn't experience meaning, purpose, peace—in a word—happiness in this life. But just where does this universal expectation for personal fulfillment come from?" he asks. "It isn't something we drum up or manufacture on our own. Rather, the burning yearning for 'what is real' is incorporated into our design. This burning can lead either to the torment of pain or the torrent of love. It will either consume us or consummate us."[5]

There it is: what we do with that "ache" in our bones is no small matter. It's no footnote in the grand scheme of things. What we do with our yearning is precisely what determines "the grand scheme of things" in each of our lives. What we do with eros—where we take it—will determine whether we are consumed or consummated, whether we are brought to ruin or reunion . . . with whatever that "something" is we're seeking.

## SEEKING UNION

The yearning of eros reveals that we are incomplete, and that we are in search of another to make "sense" of ourselves. Although that yearning originates deep in our souls, it's also manifested in our bodies. Our very bodies tell the story of our incompleteness: more specifically, those parts of our bodies that distinguish us as male and female.

Think about it—a man's body makes no sense by itself; and a woman's body makes no sense by itself. Seen in light of each other, the picture becomes complete: we go together! Is this merely a biological reality that resulted from a random evolution? Or might a loving God be trying to tell us something fundamental about who he is and who we are by creating us this way? Consider the possibility that human sexuality—our maleness and femaleness and the call to "completion" inherent there—is itself a message from God. Consider the idea that our bodies tell a story that reveals, as we learn how to read it, the very meaning of existence and the path to the ultimate satisfaction of our deepest desires.

From the Christian point of view, our creation as male and female is a "sacramental" reality: a physical sign of something transcendent, spiritual, and even divine. In the biblical under-standing, there exists a profound unity between that which is physical and that which is spiritual.[6] This means that our bodies are not mere shells in which our true "spiritual selves" live. We are a profound unity of body and soul, matter and spirit. In a very real way, we *are* our bodies.

We can see this truth in the fact that if I were to haul off in a fit of rage and break somebody's jaw, he wouldn't sue me for property damages; he'd sue me for personal assault. Our living bodies are our living selves. And this means our bodily maleness or femaleness speaks to our deepest *identity* as persons.[7] As John Paul II observed, our bodies show us who we are and also who we are meant to be.[8]

Indeed, the moment we are born (or even sooner today with sonograms), we are personally *identified* by our sex organs. "It's a boy!" or "It's a girl!" And as this sexual identity develops and matures it expresses itself as an undeniable cry of the heart for completeness. Who doesn't remember the tumultuous years of puberty, when that sense of "incompleteness" is awakened and the yearning of eros (in the specifically sexual sense) presents itself with all its angst and mayhem?

The poetry, myths, and literature of the whole world ex-plore this link between sexuality and man's quest for "some-thing more"—for completeness, happiness, fulfillment. In ancient philosophy, Plato believed that the human being was originally spherical and complete in himself but was later split in two by the god Zeus as a punishment for pride. Plato said that men and women were constantly seeking their "other half," longing to rediscover their original integrity.

In the Judeo-Christian perspective the division of the human race into two sexes is not a result of punishment but is part of the original and "very good" design of the world. Still, in the biblical narrative "the idea is certainly present that man is somehow incomplete, driven by nature to seek in another the part that can make him whole, the idea that only in communion with the opposite sex can he become 'complete.' The biblical account thus concludes with a prophecy about Adam: 'Therefore a man leaves his father and his mother and cleaves to his wife and they become one flesh' (Gen. 2:24)."⁹ In other words, man finds a certain completion in giving himself fully to woman, and woman in giving herself fully to man—a gift so intimate that the two become "one flesh."

## EROS: YEARNING FOR INFINITY

In the New Testament we learn that this "prophecy about Adam" was ultimately a prophecy about the "New Adam," Christ the Bridegroom, who would leave his Father in heaven to become "one flesh" with his Bride, the Church (see Eph. 5:31–32). What an astounding proclamation! The Christian faith proclaims not only that God loves us, but that God loves us in such an intimate way that the Scripture compares that love to the love of husband and wife in their most intimate embrace. In fact, God made us as sexual beings—as men and women with a desire for union—precisely to tell the story of his love for us. In the biblical view, the fulfillment of love between the sexes is a great foreshadowing of something quite literally "out of this world"—the infinite bliss and ecstasy that awaits us in heaven. As Pope Benedict XVI put it, erotic love is meant to provide "not just fleeting pleasure, but also a certain foretaste of the pinnacle of our existence, of that beatitude [blissful happiness] for which our whole being yearns."[10]

"We talk about different 'sexual orientations' in human life," says Lorenzo Albacete, a physicist turned Catholic priest and a beloved professor of mine. "But the ultimate orientation of human sexuality is the human heart's yearning for infinity. Human sexuality, therefore, is a sign of eternity."[11] This means sex is not just about sex. As we learn to "read" the story our bodies tell as male and female, we discover that sex is meant to point the way to the ultimate fulfillment of our every desire. Now, let me clarify—this is *not* to say that sexual activity is itself our ultimate fulfillment. That's the major mistake the world is making today. When we aim our desire for infinity at something less than infinity (like sex), we're inevitably left wanting, disillusioned, and disappointed. But, again, sex *is* meant to be a sign, a foreshadowing of ultimate fulfillment.

In short, that combustible force called eros is meant to be the fuel that launches our rocket toward the infinite. And from this perspective it's all the more meaningful that NASA scientists launched Beethoven's "ode to longing" out into the far reaches of the galaxy—looking, hoping, groping, perhaps, for some answer to the question *What are we human beings looking for?* What are we to do with that deep ache we feel inside for "something"?

It seems to me we have three choices, three offerings held out by three distinct "gospels." The word "gospel," of course, means "good news." Everyone is searching for some "good news," some promise of happiness. Each of the three "gospels" that I'll outline in this book offers a promise of happiness determined by a specific orientation of our desire, a specific invitation for how to direct or how to deal with our hunger. I put "gospel" in quotes, however, because not every promise held out to us is truly good news. Each of the three "gospels" purports to be good news, but it's up to us to test each one, poke holes in it, see if it holds water, see if it pans out. I call these "gospels":

GOSPEL #1: the starvation diet

GOSPEL #2: fast food

GOSPEL #3: the banquet

These different "gospels" lay claim to our love and allegiance by orienting our desire in a given direction. And the direction we choose to direct our desire will determine our approach to, well, pretty much everything. If we are seeking happiness, the question is this: Is our desire directed toward that which truly satisfies, toward that which truly fulfills? If not, we will need to redirect our desire toward that which *does* satisfy, or, at least to that gospel that offers a trustworthy *hope* of satisfaction. In short, if we are to find satisfaction of that universal human longing, we must learn how to direct our *desire* according to God's *design* so that it launches us to our *destiny*. That's the journey on which this book invites you.

# CHAPTER 2

# THE STARVATION DIET

*That's me in the spotlight*
*Losing my religion*
—R.E.M.[1]

I had no idea as a kid that my internally combustible attraction to the girl sitting next to me in class or my desire to run home, climb my favorite tree, and listen to my transistor radio had anything to do with God. Admittedly, my thoughts about girls and the music I listened to didn't always lead me in holy directions. And yet even misdirected eros shows us the kind of beings we are—creatures of desire who long for life, for beauty, for freedom, for adventure, for intimacy, for affirmation, for love and union.

It's unfortunate but true that what we learn about Christianity in our upbringing rarely connects the dots for us between what we feel and desire in our hearts and what Christianity holds out to us. More often than not, eros is often considered the enemy of holiness whereas a list of burdensome rules and rote prayers are presented as the means to it. John Eldredge laments that the way

> Christianity is often presented . . . could not seem more ir-relevant to our deepest desires . . . Regardless of where you go to church, there is nearly always an unspoken list of what you shouldn't do (tailored to your denomination and culture, but typically rather long) and a list of what you may do (usually much shorter—mostly religious activity that seems totally unrelated to our deepest desires . . .). And this, we are told, is the good news. Know the right thing; do the right thing. This is life?[2]

No. This is *not* life. Life—the life Christ came to give us "to the full" (John 10:10)—is a wedding feast: a feast of love, joy, delight, bliss, and ecstasy beyond all telling. It's called heaven. And all the beauty and joys of creation sing of this wedding feast, point to it, predict it, and are meant to prepare us for it—especially our own creation as sexual beings (male and female) and the vehement flame of eros that draws us together as one.

In my lectures over the years, I've asked countless thousands these questions: *How many of you were raised in a Christian home?* Nearly everyone in my audience raises their hands. Then I ask: *How many of you would say that in your Christian upbringing there was open, honest, normal, healthy conversation about God's glorious, beautiful, wonderful plan for making us male and female; and how many of you learned growing up that the one flesh union is meant to be a foreshadowing of the eternal ecstasy and bliss that awaits us in heaven?* Consistently, I get about a 1 to 2 percent response.

If these numbers are a fair representation, this means that—when it comes to the hunger of eros—about 98 to 99 percent of us were raised on what I call the "starvation diet gospel" (or at least a significantly "malnourished" gospel). I hope it was never actually stated this way, but the general message hanging in the air for a lot of people raised in Christian homes was this: *Your desires (especially your sexual desires) are bad, and they will only get you in trouble. So you need to repress, ignore, or otherwise annihilate them. But follow all of these rules and you'll be a good, upstanding Christian citizen.*

## LIFELESS LEGALISM

This isn't Christianity. This is stoicism. This is lifeless legalism. To kill our desires is "suicide of the soul." This "tragedy is increased tenfold when this suicide . . . is committed under the conviction that this is precisely what Christianity recommends. We have never been more mistaken."[3]

I'm convinced that this stoic brand of religion is responsible for the fact that large numbers of people raised in Christian homes in the western world have abandoned their faith as adults. In practice, legalism and moralism can make people want to run in precisely the other direction—indulging in anything and everything and inviting others to do the same. Take pop singer Madonna, for example. This modern icon of sexual "liberation" was raised, as she says, "in a very Catholic house." And her reflections on her religious upbringing echo the sentiments of a large swath of the population: "So religion was a big part of my life—going to school, reading the Bible, praying to Jesus, going to confession, thinking about good, bad, what's a sin, what's an original sin, what's a venial sin, but that's all morals and ethics," she says.

Why did she grow up wanting to break all the rules? She insists: "Because the rules didn't make sense, that's why." They "don't answer the bigger questions . . . I never really got a lot of my questions answered, so consequently, I just sort of moved away from religion . . . I don't reject the idea that Jesus Christ walked on this earth, and He was a divine being," says Madonna, "but I reject the religious behavior of any religious organization that does not encourage you to ask questions and do your own exploration."[4]

I'm certainly not endorsing the direction in which Madonna took her "seeking." Rather, I'm lamenting the fact that she was raised with a terribly truncated sense of the life Christ holds out to us. Hence, she took her questions elsewhere. And who can't understand why? If Christianity is understood as merely a legalistic adherence to a moral code that makes no allowance for a person's seeking, why would anyone want to continue practicing such a vapid religiosity? Jesus didn't come to squelch our seeking. He encouraged us to ask, to seek, and to knock. "For everyone who asks receives; the one who seeks finds; and to the one who knocks, the door will be opened" (Matt. 7:8). The first words placed in the mouth of Christ in John's Gospel are not "Follow all these rules or you're going to hell." Rather, Christ probes our hearts with a question: "What are you looking for?" (John 1:38). As we'll discuss at length throughout this book, Christ wants us to live courageously from our deepest, most ardent desires—not to stifle them. What's needed to progress on the journey of the Christian life is *depth* of desire, not *death* of desire.

## THE "BEAST" WITHIN

Those who see desire itself as the enemy of the Christian life have a very skewed notion of Christianity and their own humanity. They're typically locked in a pessimistic, suspicious view of the human heart as "utterly depraved" and, thus, incapable of desiring and choosing good. Although some of the first Protestant reformers held this idea, as have some Catholic thinkers, the Church has never believed this.[5] This bleak and inherently suspicious view of human life is actually a heresy known as Jansenism, which has been repeatedly condemned by the Church. We are, of course, affected deeply by original sin, and we must engage in a lively battle at times against an interior inclination to abuse good things. But we are not powerless to resist temptation, and, with the help of grace, we can learn to "untwist" what sin has twisted in us in order to reclaim all that is true, good, and beautiful.

Cornelius Jansen, a sixteenth-century Flemish bishop, believed that people were utterly powerless to resist temptation. His teaching—which spread through the seminary system in Europe and then to America—cast a shadow of suspicion over, well, everything, creating an oppressive scrupulosity that still passes today in the minds of many as "the Christian way."

The warped Jansenist form of religion is humorously caricatured in a scene from the 1985 film *Heaven Help Us,* set in an all-boys Catholic high school in the mid-1960s. In one particular scene the young men of Saint Basil's are quite riled up in the presence of "the Virgin Martyr Girls," who have come for the high school mixer (search "Heaven Help Us mixer" on YouTube for a good laugh). At the start of the dance, the uptight Father Abruzzi—played by Wallace Shawn, the lispy actor who gave us the famous "in-con-scchhievable" line in *The Princess Bride*—lectures the students as follows:

> You're all at an age now when you're perHAPs beginning to notice the difference between the boys and the girls. And just as she is in every other important moment of your life, the Church is here to GUIDE you. Many of you will be experiencing certain [pause] feelings, feelings which you might be inclined to confuse with love. But, ladies and gentlemen, never confuse *love* with the DEADliest of the seven deadly sins! . . . Lust is the *beast within YOU! The beast that wants to consume you and then SPIT you out into the eternal fires of HELL,*

*where for all eternity ... your blood will boil, your bones
will burn, and your marrow will be reduced to a puTRID
BLACK SLIME!! And for what? For a few moments of
weakness that led you to admire the shape of somebody's
buttocks. [pause] Any questions?*

## WRONG MUSIC

I wouldn't suspect that anyone actually received a lecture as over-
the-top as this. The point of caricature, of course, is to exaggerate
for comic effect but in the process to make a point. This humor-
ous scene makes the same point Pope Benedict XVI made when
he lamented that people have been "warped and intimidated" by
Jansenism and by other forms of rigorism and negative appraisals
of sexuality that have found their way into the Church.[6]

But we can also acknowledge that some of what Father
Abruzzi says in his lithpy lecture is actually true. For example,
it *is* very important that we not confuse lust with love. And the
Church really *is* here to guide us in these important questions.
But even where his words might be right, his manner of present-
ing them is still *way* off.

When the words are true but their presentation is off, it's a
case of what I call: right words, *wrong* music. And what affects the
heart more, the words or the melody? We may have been given
"correct" teaching in our Christian upbringings, but if it was set to
the wrong "music" —that is, if Christian teaching was presented in
a dry, cold, mechanical, doctrinaire way, for example—our hearts
didn't (and even couldn't) respond openly and positively. No

matter how awesome the characters and the plot line, if a movie has an abrasive sound track, you'll still want to leave the theater.

Over time, of course, the pendulum swings in the other direction. Today many Christian denominations (and various groups within the Catholic Church) have adjusted not only the music, but the actual content of Christ's teaching as well. They may be singing a more welcoming tune, but it's not a genuine song if it's watering down the truth about what it means to be human. This approach, too, creates its own kind of "starvation."

What we're starved for in the "starvation diet gospel" is the *beauty* of the truth. When Christian teaching is presented without beauty, the heart is turned off and shuts down, even if what's being presented is true. Worse still, when Christian teaching is set to an "ugly tune," so to speak—for example, when the presentation of truth is tinged with self-righteousness, condemnation, accusation, or judgmentalism—the truth can come across as an affront to our hearts. And when this happens, our hearts revolt—with good reason: we're made for beauty. We must have it. We yearn for it. And when the version of Christianity that is presented to us doesn't supply what we're looking for, we seek it elsewhere.

I'm not suggesting that people's rejection of the Gospel is always the result of not having had it presented attractively enough. Christ himself presented the Gospel in precisely the right way and the people of his day still crucified him. That said, it remains true that a lot of people reject Christianity without having heard the full beauty of it.

When we're starved for beauty, something dangerous

happens. As with an unfed dog, our hunger can become raven-ous. If, on the one hand, we *scorn* truth without beauty, on the other hand, we *porn* beauty without truth. By this I mean we re-duce beauty to the merely physical level—cut off from any higher truth—and fixate on idealized images of "perfect physical beauty" for the sake of a selfish, base gratification. When this is our ap-proach to feeding eros, we're missing the divine banquet we're created for and settling for "fast food."

CHAPTER 3

# FAST FOOD

*Watch each one reach for creature comfort*
*For the filling of their holes*
—PETER GABRIEL[1]

A person can starve himself for only so long before the choice becomes clear: either I find something to eat, or . . . I'm gonna die. The hunger of eros eventually becomes so painful that the prospect of relief—wherever it can be found—trumps all fear of "breaking the rules."

This is why the culture's "fast-food gospel"—the promise of immediate gratification through indulgence of desire—inevitably wins large numbers of converts from the "starvation diet gospel." I don't know about you, but if the only two choices are starvation or greasy chicken nuggets, I'm going for the nuggets.

Like most people raised in Catholic schools in the '70s and '80s, I wasn't getting my questions answered. And I had lots of them, especially about sex. So I looked for answers elsewhere—and the culture's "fast-food" offering filled a void. Eating from this menu caught up with me in my college years. In fact, I ended up like the guy in the movie *Super Size Me* (2004)—the documentary by Morgan Spurlock who ate every meal at McDonald's for thirty days to see what would happen to him. By the end of his little experiment, he was dying—his body was literally shutting down from all the grease and sodium he had consumed. That's a fairly accurate picture of how I felt inside in my early twenties.

Let's face it, there's something in us that can be very attracted to the promise of happiness through noncommitted, pregnancy-free sexual indulgence. It's a false promise, of course. For in the end, the "fast-food gospel" isn't a gospel at all. Like the starvation diet, it leads to death—not by malnutrition, but by poisoning our system with unhealthy food.

Even so, in a way, its proponents are still on to something. The fast-food gospel mimics the banquet we're created for. *That's* why fast food can be so attractive. You see, there's something the secular culture "gets" about us as human beings that the Jansenistic moralizers of the world don't: eros is not something that needs to be repressed; it's something that needs to be fed. *What* we feed it is another matter, of course. But eros *must* be given hope of satisfaction. To the Father Abruzzis of the world, the idea that eros must be given hope of satisfaction is, shall we say, "in-con-scchhievable!"

## IS VICTORIA IN ON AUGUSTINE'S SECRET?

Saint Augustine was a man who knew what it was to pine and ache and burn inside. He felt desire so ardently and wrote about it so poignantly that I like to call him "the doctor of desire." In fact, he maintained that the "whole life of the good Christian is a holy longing . . . That is our life, to be trained by longing"[2]—to follow the heart's deepest desire where it ultimately takes us.

Understanding the human person in this way—as a creature of ardent desire—gives us new (and perhaps more compassionate) eyes to see what is going on all around us in today's hyper-eroticized culture. In a marvelously insightful book called *Desiring the Kingdom*, philosophy professor James K. A. Smith suggests that the culture's focus on sex and desire is not all bad. Even though the entertainment and marketing industries warp and misdirect eros (often terribly so), they're still on to something.

Neuromarketers—those who study brain activity to gauge people's response to marketing stimuli—report that the most effective advertisements and movie trailers are the ones that activate the part of the brain associated with desire, craving, and sex.[3] Not surprising if we understand what makes the human being tick. In marketing we find the promise of a kind of transcendence that's linked to what James K. A. Smith calls a "bastardization of the erotic." Advertisers are well-schooled in the movements of our hearts. They know how to appeal directly to eros, and then, through substitution, they channel our yearning into their product—or at least associate their product with our desire and for only "three easy payments of $19.95" offer "satisfaction guaranteed."

Anyone raised in our culture can think of endless examples of this bait and switch, but Smith singles out Victoria's Secret as a particularly interesting case because of the way in which the company's advertising reaches out to (and into) the longings of both men and women. Victoria's Secret commercials appeal to men for obvious reasons, so the company advertises during football games for the same reason that kids' cereals advertise during Saturday morning cartoons. And yet few men shop at Victoria's Secret. But just as Kellogg's knows kids will ask their parents for what they saw on TV, Victoria's Secret knows men will ask women for the same. And because women want to be desired by men, they'll shop at Victoria's Secret. The "secret" here is the direct appeal to *desire*.

The common "churchy" response to all this is predictable enough: put a lid on it; the sexual passion coursing through the culture must be quelled. But Smith suggests that Victoria's Secret might actually be right (or at least on to something) just where that repressive rigorism that passes for Christianity has been wrong. He elaborates:

> More specifically, I think we should first recognize and admit that the marketing industry—which promises an erotically charged transcendence through media that connect to our heart and imagination—is operating with a better, more creational, more incarnational, more holistic anthropology than much of the [Christian world]. In other words, I think we must admit

that the marketing industry is able to capture, form, and direct our desires precisely because they have rightly discerned that we are embodied, desiring creatures whose [hearts are] governed by the imagination. Marketers have figured out the way to our heart because they "get it": they rightly understand that, at root, we are *erotic* creatures—creatures who are oriented primarily by love and passion and desire. In sum, I think Victoria is in on Augustine's secret.[4]

Smith's point is important. He's certainly *not* condoning the soft porn of Victoria's Secret (nor am I!). Rather, he's challenging Christians to recognize that, although the marketing industry blatantly misdirects human desire, it still understands that we are *embodied creatures of desire*. This was Augustine's secret: "Our life is a gymnasium of desire," he said.[5] The question, as always, is what do we *do* with our desire? Where do we take it? Do the promises of the "fast-food gospel" really pan out? Sex, sex, and more sex—this, we are told, is what we want? This is happiness? This is satisfaction? Really? Do we truly think the reason Mick Jagger "can't get no satisfaction" is that he's not having enough sex?

I look around at the culture and see evidence that there is *plenty* of sex going on, but very little happiness. Sigmund Freud himself reflected on "the possibility that something in the nature of the sexual instinct itself is unfavorable to the realization of complete satisfaction."[6] Maybe that "something" is the fact that sex is a *finite* reality, and we're meant for something *infinite*. Sex hints at the infinite, and (from the Christian point of view) is meant to point us to it and even allow us to participate in it, but it seems we often mistake the hint for the reality hinted at. And when we take our desire for the infinite and try to satisfy it with something finite, we are *always* left wanting.

## REDUCTION OF DESIRE

If eros is ultimately a yearning for the infinite, then we clearly miss the mark when we seek ultimate satisfaction of eros in finite things. And when we miss the mark, we sin (the Hebrew word for sin, *hattah*, means "to miss the mark"). The fast-food gospel actually forces us to *reduce* eros (as if that were possible), to limit desire and direct it to something less—something infinitely less—than what we're really looking for. What leads us to the fast food, then, is not that we desire too much but that we desire too little! As C. S. Lewis put it:

> Indeed, if we consider the unblushing promises of reward and the staggering nature of the rewards promised in the Gospels, it would seem that Our Lord finds our desires not too strong, but too weak. We are half-hearted creatures, fooling about with drink and sex and ambition when infinite joy is offered us, like an ignorant child who wants to go on making mud pies in a slum because he cannot imagine what is meant by the offer of a holiday at the sea. We are far too easily pleased.[7]

It seems we are far too easily pleased, far too easily taken in by the "fast food," because so few of us have ever even heard about the blissful satisfaction of eros promised us in the true Christian vision of things. Tragically, the majority of those raised in Christian homes have simply not heard the fullness of the "good news"—or at least not in a way that penetrated our hearts and engaged our erotic core, that place inside us that burns, not with pornographic lust, but with a *noble* eros. We all have our battles with the selfish pull of lust, but we all experience a noble eros also—that unquenchable yearning for love, for affirmation, for union, intimacy, joy, and fulfillment. Eros in this understanding, as Pope Benedict XVI put it, is the desire within us that "seeks God."[8]

When the distinctions are never made between the distortions of eros on the one hand (what we might call "eroticism"), and the aspirations of a true, noble eros on the other, eros is condemned by the "righteous" and its distortions are celebrated by the "sinners." Let's face it, lacking any other place to take that "fire" within, many people see sex as the most powerful and attractive experience life has to offer—and far more fulfilling than anything "religion" seems to offer. Even in its distorted expressions, sex still hints at something we crave; it still offers some semblance of joy and happiness. Even in its cheapened and loveless expressions, sex still offers at least a momentary escape from the pressures and burdens of life. All of this led Woody Allen to quip, "Sex without love is a meaningless experience, but as far as meaningless experiences go, it's pretty damn good."[9]

Yes, the fast-food gospel *can* seem "pretty damn good." But in the end, frauds never pan out. The semblance of joy and happiness is not enough. Loveless indulgence of erotic desire can't possibly reach us where we yearn to be reached, where the questions continue to gnaw at us, where the cry of the heart remains as haunting as ever. Even Hollywood is beginning to ask questions about the consequences of our sexual choices. Recent films like *Friends with Benefits*, *No Strings Attached*, and *Crazy, Stupid, Love* all ask the question: Is the semblance of satisfaction offered by uncommitted sex really what we're looking for? Even *Playboy* mogul Hugh Hefner admits that despite countless "lovers," he has "never known a fulfillment of love."[10]

Is there such a fulfillment?

Kiss me with the kisses of your mouth, for your love is more delightful than wine . . . The King has taken me into the wine cellar . . . He has taken me to the banquet hall, and his banner over me is love . . . (Song 1:2,4; 2:4)

# CHAPTER 4

# THE BANQUET

*Think about it, there must be a higher love*
*Down in the heart or hidden in the stars above*
—STEVE WINWOOD[1]

The Prophet Isaiah declares: "The Lord will prepare a lavish banquet for all, a feast of rich food and pure, choice wines; juicy, rich food, and pure, choice wines" (Isa. 25:6). I love this imagery because, well, I *love* to eat. Love it! Have you ever pondered how absolutely amazing our taste buds are? These tiny sensory organs bring such delight! A gooey Cinnabon at the airport, or a warm, buttery Auntie Anne's soft pretzel; better yet—one of my wife's delicious soups, pasta dishes, or her homemade cappuccino cheesecake with cinnamon graham cracker crust. What a treat! And when it's over . . . what a disappointment.

I hate it when a delicious meal is over. Why? Well, because . . . *it's over.* Despite the manners my parents taught me, I delight in licking the plate of every last schmear of gravy, or pasta sauce, or cinnamon-crumbly-goodness to extend the delight as long as possible, but ultimately I have to face the fact that this time of pleasure has come to an abrupt end. And I'm sad about that. *I don't want this joy to stop—ever!* Translation: I'm looking for a feast that lasts *forever* . . . Is there such a thing? If there is, it's certainly beyond anything this life has to offer. And that means that, while I'm here in this life, I have to figure out what to do with this painful ache.[2]

Right in that moment of sadness, at the end of the meal, it seems I have three options:

(1) I can repress my desire in hopes of alleviating the sadness;

(2) I can gluttonously indulge my desire in more food than my body needs; or

(3) I can let the deliciousness of the meal and the sadness that it's over do its job: to awaken my hope in and whet my appetite for the life to which I'm destined, the life beyond this life where the banquet never ends.

The option I choose in that moment indicates whether I'm learning to direct my *desire* according to God's *design* so that it launches me to my *destiny*. In short, the option I choose in that moment determines whether I'm on the path of a stoic, an addict, or a mystic.

## STOIC, ADDICT, OR MYSTIC

The *stoic* tries to avoid the pain of desiring more than this life has to offer by choosing not to want so much, by shutting desire down. As a stoic, I'm afraid of the thirst in my soul to the point of not wanting to feel it, and certainly not wanting to open it up. Life's easier that way, and I can feign a certain peace: nothing really troubles me, and nothing really excites me either. But this is the unmoved "peace" of a corpse at the morgue. It's lifeless, vapid. It exchanges red-hot lifeblood for blue-cold embalming fluid. Stoics are usually very well meaning and are rightly concerned about how desires can be impure and misdirected. But rather than working to redirect desire toward its proper end, they shut desire down in favor of a "dutiful life."

The *addict*, on the other hand, tries to avoid the pain of wanting more than this life has to offer by gorging on the things this life *does* have to offer, trying to suck infinity out of finite things. But finite things, as we have discussed, can never satisfy our yearning for the infinite. Once I've attained what I thought I wanted but I'm still left wanting, what do I think I need? *More.* Then when I attain more and it still doesn't satisfy me, what do I think I need? *More* and *more* and *more* . . . This is why the fast-food gospel leads not to satisfaction and happiness, but to addiction and despair. And yet, although the addict may be on a fast track to self-destruction, at least he is in touch with his desire. As such, he holds something in common with the mystic.

The *mystic* is the one who allows himself to feel the deepest depths of human desire and chooses to "stay in the pain" of wanting more than this life has to offer. Having walked through many purifying trials (what the mystical tradition of the Church calls "dark nights"), he is able both to do without the many pleasures of this world *and* to rejoice in all the true pleasures of this world without idolizing them—that is, without trying to suck infinity out of them. As the Apostle Paul says, "I have learned the secret of being well fed and of going hungry, of living in abundance and of being in need" (Phil. 4:12).

For the mystic, the true pleasures of the world are a welcome but only dim foreshadowing of the ecstasy that awaits him in the life to come. He can live within that "ache" (what the mystical tradition calls "the wound of love") because of his living hope that his "soul shall be satisfied as with a banquet" (Ps. 63:5), a banquet that lasts forever and will fulfill his every desire beyond all earthly imaginings.

The truth is, we're all called to be "mystics." And that means we're all called to enter into the "great mystery" of Christ and his mad love affair with us. We often think of the Christian mystics as those saints who experience phenomena like bodily levitations or the bleeding wounds of Christ. That's extraordinary mysticism, and few are called to that. But there is an "ordinary mysticism" to which we are all called, an ongoing encounter with the "Mystery" in and through the normal day-to-day circumstances of life. This isn't something we have to go searching for among the clouds. For "God comes to us in the things we know best and can verify most easily, the things of our everyday life, apart from which we cannot understand ourselves."[3]

A mystic is someone who is able to "taste and see the goodness of the Lord" in all of life's circumstances and events, and in all of his creation, even amidst trials and sufferings. A mystic is someone who has been captivated by the fragrance and beauty of divine love, and nothing can thwart his or her desire for ever deeper intimacy with the Divine Lover. "God calls us all to this intimate union with him," states the *Catechism of the Catholic Church* (the Catholic Church's official collection of doctrine on faith and morals), "even if the special graces or extraordinary signs of this mystical life are granted only to some for the sake of manifesting the gratuitous gift given to all."[4]

In short, a mystic is someone who has entered God's love song, hears it everywhere, and can't help but dance because of it. What is God's love song? It would have to be the greatest song imaginable, the song of all songs. It is. It's the Song of Songs: the Bible's great ode to *eros*.

Saints have written more commentaries on this unabashedly erotic poetry than on any other book in the Bible. More than on the Gospels. More than on all of Saint Paul's letters. Why? What do the saints know that the rest of us need to get in on? If the

Gospels are "the heart of all the Scriptures,"[5] the mystics point us to the Song of Songs as "the essence of biblical faith."[6] This is where, in a very particular way, the "divine nectar" can be accessed and savored. This is where we gain entrance to the divine "wedding feast," to the "banquet hall of love" (see Song 2:4). This is where we can surrender to the ecstasy and bliss for which we yearn. In short, to the scandal and dismay of the Father Abruzzis of this world, the saints teach us that this biblical ode to eros is the *authentic soundtrack of Christianity*.

## THE RELIGION OF DESIRE AND ECSTASY

If we believe the Jansenistic perspective to be the authentically Christian one, we might expect the first chapter of the *Catechism of the Catholic Church* to begin with a statement about what wretched sinners we are and how angry God is with us. Instead, section one of Chapter 1 of the *Catechism* begins with a statement on human desire—what it is, why we have it, and where it leads. It states: "The desire for God is written in the human heart, because man is created by God and for God; and God never ceases to draw man to himself. Only in God will he find the truth and happiness he never stops searching for: The dignity of man rests above all on the fact that he is called to communion with God."[7]

In other words, the "ache" we feel in our bones is a yearning for God. In fact, when Christians say the word "God," what do we mean? It's the word we use, says Saint Augustine, to describe "all that we yearn for."[8] As the psalmist cries: "O God, you are my

God, for you I long; for you my soul is thirsting. My body pines for you like a dry, weary land without water" (Ps. 63:1).

The *Catechism* goes on to discuss various ways this yearning has found expression throughout history, including how our desire for God can get off track. It mentions, among other things, the "bad example" of some believers (starvation diet) and the lure of the "riches of this world" (fast food) that can cause us to forget, overlook, or explicitly reject our call to union with God. Then this section of the *Catechism* ends with Saint Augustine's famous words to God: "you have made us for yourself, and our heart is restless until it rests in you."[9]

"In this creative restlessness beats and pulsates what is most deeply human," wrote John Paul II.[10] This restless yearning is what makes us "religious beings." And religion "is either the reasonable quest for the satisfaction of all the original desires of the heart," says Lorenzo Albacete, "or it is a dangerous, divisive, harmful waste of time."[11]

These are strong words worth reflecting upon. How seriously do we take our quest for the satisfaction of the deepest desires of our hearts? Are we even in touch with these desires? Have we mistaken the superficial satisfaction of physical pleasure (the fast-food approach) with the much deeper satisfaction of the soul we crave? Have we reduced religion to a dutiful following of the rules (the starvation diet approach)? In short, if a Christian is not passionately pursuing the satisfaction of his deepest yearnings, then he's not really following Christ. He may be following an ethical code, and he may be a good and kind person, but his lamp isn't lit; his fire isn't burning; he's not alive.

Christianity, in particular, we must recall, is the religion that proclaims "blessed" those who hunger and thirst, for they shall be satisfied (see Matt. 5:6; Luke 6:21). Indeed, at the source and summit of Christian faith we find heavenly bread and divine wine given precisely to satisfy and even to "intoxicate" us. Whoever eats this bread and drinks this chalice will live forever. He shall not hunger, and he shall never thirst (see John 6:51, 35). He shall exclaim in communion with all the saints: "The Lord has prepared a feast for me: given wine in plenty for me to drink."[12]

In the Lord's Supper, the Church "has dressed her meat, mixed her wine, yes, she has spread her table. She has sent out her maidens; she calls from the heights out over the city: 'Let whoever is simple turn in here; to him who lacks understanding, I say, Come, eat my food, and drink the wine I have mixed!'" (Prov. 9:2–5). And as the Church offers the "meat" of the sacrificial Lamb and pours out his "wine," she proclaims in all her joy: "Blessed are those called to the supper of the Lamb!"[13]

How should we who are so blessed to be called to this supper respond? Teresa of Avila, commenting on Christ's desire to take us into the "wine cellar" of the Song of Songs,[14] exclaims: "The King seems to refuse nothing to the Bride! Well, then, let her drink as much as she desires and get drunk on all these wines in the cellar of God! Let her enjoy these joys, wonder at these great things, and not fear to lose her life through drinking much more than her weak nature enables her to do. Let her die at last in this paradise of delights; blessed death that makes one live in such a way."[15] (I don't know about you, but somehow this vision of things got left out of my Catholic schooling.)

Despite all the widespread impressions to the contrary, we must impress this truth upon our souls and allow it to settle into our bones (right where we find our deepest longings!): Christianity is the religion of desire—the religion that *redeems eros*—and its saints are the ones who have had the courage to *feel* the abyss of longing in their souls and in their bodies and to open that longing in "the groanings of prayer" to the One who alone can heal their "wound of love." In other words, the saints have learned how to open all their desires for love and union to the Love and Union that alone can satisfy: "mystical marriage" . . . *with God*. Or we could say it even more simply: the saints have learned to open eros (their yearning for love) to Eros (God's passionate love for them).

But is eros really the right word to use here? We must labor, it's true, to free this word from all lustful distortions in order to get the proper picture. As we do, we begin to see the true nobility and sacred nature of eros more clearly. Recall Pope Benedict's statement, quoted in the last chapter, that eros, at its deepest level, is the desire within us that "seeks God."[16] In turn, God's love "may certainly be called *eros*," the pope tells us, "yet it is also totally *agape*."[17]

## GOD'S "CRAZY" LOVE FOR US

"Agape" is the Greek word for "selfless love." It refers to other-centered, sacrificial giving without ulterior motives, and, since it is considered more spiritual, it is often set in sharp distinction to eros. But this is a mistake.

Father Raniero Cantalamessa, official preacher to the papal household in Rome, observed that love "suffers from ill-fated separation not only in the mentality of the secularized world, but also in that of the opposite side, among believers . . . Simplifying the situation to the greatest extent," he said, "we can articulate it thus: In the world we find eros without agape; among believers we often find agape without eros." The former "is a body without a soul" and is well understood "propagated as it is in a hammering way" by the secular media. The latter—agape without eros—"is a soul without a body"; it's a "cold love" in which "the component linked to affectivity and the heart is systematically denied or repressed." Either way, by separating eros and agape, we distort the truth of love and rupture our own humanity. For the "human being is not an angel, that is, a pure spirit; he is a soul and body substantially united: everything he does, including loving, must reflect this structure."[18]

In Christ, God himself took on a body to reveal his spiritual love *in the flesh*. Christ loves us with the love of a perfect Bridegroom—a sacrificial and other-centered outpouring of passion and "fire." This is why God's love "may certainly be called *eros*, yet it is also totally *agape*."[19]

If Christianity is the religion of wild passion and desire, this is first and foremost because Christ himself is full of wild passion and desire. From all eternity he has received the blazing love of the Father, and it is precisely that blazing love that compelled him to take on flesh in order to "set the world ablaze" (Luke 12:49). If we feel an unquenchable thirst for God, it's only because he first felt an unquenchable thirst for us. "This is love, not that we loved God, but that he first loved us" (1 John 4:10). So before he offers to quench the thirst of the woman at the well, Christ first expresses *his* thirst: "Give me a drink" (John 4:7). And in his ultimate outpouring of love from the cross, he cries: "I thirst" (John 19:28).

We must allow ourselves to "be overtaken . . . by God's 'crazy' love for us," says Pope Benedict XVI.[20] If we only knew how much Jesus thirsts for us, how compelled he is by his wild, divine Eros to pour himself out for us, to become *one* with us by offering his very body and blood as food and drink! Oh how he longs for us to satisfy our hunger with his flesh and quench our thirst with his blood . . . unto infinite intoxication! How he longs to delight in the "wedding feast" with his Bride: "I have desired with a great desire to eat this Passover with you" (Luke 22:15).

Yes, the banquet we desire is a "wedding feast"—an ecstasy of love and union only dimly foreshadowed in the ecstasy of love and union that spouses know here on earth. Yes, we are created for ecstasy: we must say it unabashedly, for that's the "good news" of the Gospel in a nutshell. As John Eldredge observes, "Christianity refuses to budge from the fact that man was made for pleasure, that his beginning and his end is a paradise, and that the goal of living is to find Life. Jesus knows the dilemma of desire, and he speaks to it in nearly everything he says . . . He knows that ecstasy is not an option; we are made for bliss, and we must have it, one way or another."[21]

Both the great sinners and the great saints know they're created for ecstasy. It's the Jansenists and other "starvation-diet subscribers" who have confused us on this point. The great sinners and the great saints, in fact, are made of the very same "stuff"—a mad, burning, aching, wild desire for ecstasy. What's the difference? The great sinners head for the fast food while the great saints have discovered the living hope of the banquet.

And this, it seems, helps explain why great sinners are often the ones who become great saints. They may have been eating from the wrong menu, but at least they're in touch with their hunger, so when the banquet shows up, they're often the first to recognize that that's what they've been looking for all along. Those who subscribe to the "starvation diet," on the other hand, aren't even in touch with their hunger enough to know what it means to be invited to the feast. This is why the addict, in a real way, is closer to the mystic than is the stoic. As Saint Augustine is often cited as saying: "He who loses himself in his passion is less lost than he who loses his passion."[22] Of course, whether one subscribes to the fast-food or to the starvation diet, everyone is invited to the banquet. But those in the habit of repressing their hunger have the extra step to make of reawakening and reacquainting themselves with their heart's deepest desires. And that can be scary. Ardent desires tend to disrupt the "dutiful life." They topple the apple cart, and, because ardent desires can be misleading, starvation-diet subscribers tend to view them primarily as a threat and as an "occasion of sin."

Ardent desires can be an occasion of sin. It's true. Diving headlong into pursuing our desires without wise guidance and proper discernment will, for sure, stir up a hornet's nest and get us in trouble, especially if we have grown accustomed to indulging our desires in the "fast food." But does that mean the solution is to ignore, repress, or otherwise annihilate our desires? That would be suicide of the soul. Eventually *we must learn how to open our desires up* and direct them toward the mystical ecstasy for which we're created. "For no one is in any way disposed for . . . mystical ecstasy," Saint Bonaventure tells us, "unless . . . he is a *man of desires*."[23]

## "I'M FEARFUL OF MY JOY"

The interior battle we experience with our desires is pointedly captured in the Academy Award–winning film *Babette's Feast* (1987). I encourage you not only to watch this movie, but to study it. It's sympathetic to the human struggle, the temptation we face either to squelch desire in the name of "virtue" or to indulge desire in the name of "happiness." But in the end, the movie gently reveals the way of conversion from both "the starvation diet" and the "fast-food diet" to "the banquet." It shows us that it is possible to overcome our fears and our addictions and enter the feast rejoicing.

The movie is set in a desolate corner of Denmark in the late 1800s and tells the story of two elderly sisters named Martine and Filippa who keep the memory of their "well-respected and perhaps a little feared" father alive among the aging congregants of a strict religious sect he had founded. Babette first appears in the film as the congregation sings: "Never would you give a stone to the child who begs for bread," presaging her role as the one who would help the people to exchange their piously chosen stones for the heavenly banquet. And the presence of this rather elegant French woman among such austere Danes can be explained, the narrator tells us, "only through the hidden regions of the heart." Ah, that's the key! Access to the heavenly feast comes only through the hidden regions of the heart.

The story then takes us back nearly fifty years to a time when Martine's and Filippa's beauty was likened "to flowering fruit trees." They were never seen at local balls or parties, so young men went to church to see them. Among their father's flock, however, "earthly love and marriage were considered to be of scant worth, and merely empty illusion." Not surprisingly, these two young beauties upset "the peace of heart and the destinies" of two men, both of whom came from "the great world outside."

Lorens, the visiting nephew of a devotee of the pastor, upon meeting Martine had "a mighty vision of a higher and purer life" than the one he was living as a rogue officer in the Swedish cavalry. He tried to win her heart while attending church meetings but couldn't break through her austere shell. He gave up despondently and devoted himself to a life of military ambition and worldly indulgence.

Filippa was pursued by a famous French opera singer named Papin. Mesmerized by Filippa's voice, he was convinced that if she followed his training her singing would "surely save souls" and "comfort the poor." At one point, as her sister and father listen disapprovingly from another room, Filippa and Papin sing a duet from Mozart's opera *Don Giovanni*. As the lover in that story passionately pursues his beloved, it becomes clear that Papin is not merely acting the part. He has fallen for Filippa, and through the song he expresses his desire to make her his wife. Trembling, yet listening, Filippa sings:

> I'm fearful of my joy
> Desire, love, and doubting are battling in my heart.

By the end of the song, Filippa has allowed herself to be wooed and is daring to *feel* her desire, daring to hope in love's fulfillment. But alas, just when we're rooting for Filippa to break out of her prison and follow Papin's passion and her own to the altar, the next scene reveals her chosen spouse: she has wed herself to fear and sends Papin away.

We often do the same with God, don't we? Like Papin, Christ sings of his passionate desire for us, his heart bleeding with a divine Eros. And, like Filippa, we tremble yet listen. We yearn, but we're afraid of allowing our eros to open up to Eros. Christ wants to set us on *fire*, but we're afraid to burn. Heavenly bliss is our most ardent desire. But we're fearful of our own joy. Desire, love, and doubting are battling in our hearts.

Perhaps we're afraid of how ardent is our own *need* for joy, and, perhaps more so, we're afraid it will never be fulfilled (filled-full). What a wild thing is that desire that incessantly aggravates the core of our being. It can scare the heck out of us. In those moments when we sense how deep the hunger goes, when we sense how needy we are and how utter our poverty—and, thus, how completely dependent we are on something outside ourselves to meet that need—we freak out. We cope either by trying to shut desire down (stoicism/starvation diet), or by seeking to fill it up on our own terms with things that never can meet our need (addiction/fast food).

Filippa felt her eros rising up, and she almost was ready to say yes to it, to give joy a chance to flourish. But, in the end, fear took over. Some would probably argue that she was right to "shut it down," or at least she was right to want to keep her desires under control, since our desires are so often out of order. This is true. Let me say it again very clearly: this side of original sin, our desires *are* very often disordered, and that means we can't simply "go with them" without some measure of caution and discernment. But "control" of our desires is not our ultimate goal.

As Father Simon Tugwell observes, "Our appetites need to be controlled because they are out of tune, out of harmony with our need for God. But control is only a temporary measure. The ideal is for us not to control our appetites at all, but to allow them full rein in the wake of an uncontrolled appetite for God."[24] G. K. Chesterton put it this way: "And the more I considered Christianity, the more I found that while it had established a rule and order, the chief aim of that order was to give room for good things to run wild."[25]

## VERTICAL WILDNESS

Letting good things run wild is what I call "vertical wildness." We have wild desires in us because we're made to "go wild" with God, in God. The saints speak of this as a kind of "divine madness" or "holy intoxication." Take this desire to "go wild" horizontally (that is, to the things of this world), and you end up at a frat party. But aim it heavenward (easier said than done), and you end up launching into infinity.

Do you remember that old Steppenwolf song "Born to Be Wild"? Yes, yes we were. We are created, as the song goes, to *"take the world in a love embrace"* and to *"fire all of our guns at once / and explode into space."*[26] And here, the members of Steppenwolf, like so many other rock musicians, show themselves to be what I call "twisted mystics." They're looking in their gut and expressing in song, in unedited fashion, what they really feel going on inside them. And, sure, it may be twisted up. Most rock music is (because most of what goes on inside us is). But untwist it and you catch a glimpse of something mystical: we *are* born to be wild; we *are* born to give ourselves whole and entire to something, surrendering all control to the wild abyss that is God.

The Jansenists would have us believe that our nature is so corrupted by sin that every human desire is suspect and thus our only dutiful response to desire is to apply the brakes. But if this is our approach to desire—always to say "no" to it—there is the danger that we will not know how to say "yes" to what God wants to lavish on us. Quoting Father Tugwell once again, "Though we may, from time to time, have to brake firmly to stop ourselves rushing headlong into silly satisfactions . . . we must not make braking a whole way of life. It is more important, eventually, to know how to say 'Yes' to a desire, than to know how to say 'No.' At the end we shall have to surrender ourselves utterly and recklessly and without any inhibition to the overwhelming attractiveness of God."[27]

The Lord calls us to "open wide" our mouths so he can fill them (see Ps. 81:10). For he has "prepared a banquet" for us (see Ps. 23:5) and he yearns ardently for us to "taste and see" that he is good (see Ps. 34:8). But, as with the rigid congregation in *Babette's Feast*, fear and "propriety" often cause us to numb our tongues. We can even confuse the good things of God for something evil, as do the sisters in the movie.

## AS IF WE NEVER HAD A SENSE OF TASTE

Martine and Filippa never marry. Now elderly, their lives are forever changed when the elegant Babette appears at their door as a refugee from the war in France. She presents the sisters with a letter from Papin who asks if they would take her in as their housekeeper. Papin's letter also laments the fate that kept Filippa's voice from filling the Grand Opera House in Paris. He expresses a heartfelt hope, however, that in paradise, he will hear her voice again: "There you will forever be the great artist that God intended you to be. Oh how you will enchant the angels." Then Papin's letter shifts abruptly: "Babette can cook . . ." But we know not how *exquisitely* until later in the story.

After several years of preparing plain, stark meals for the sisters, Babette wins a large sum of money in the French lottery and offers to provide "a real French dinner" at an upcoming celebration in honor of their long deceased father. They initially refuse, but Babette insists: "Do you hear my prayer today? It comes from my heart."

When multiple crates of exotic ingredients arrive, the sisters are plagued by their worst fears. Martine warns the congregation that Babette's feast may actually be a "satanic Sabbath" that could expose them to "evil powers." They all agree to fall silent at the table and numb their tongues: "It will be just as if we never had a sense of taste," they say.

They don't realize, however, that Martine's long-lost suitor, Lorens, will be present at the celebration. As the feast unfolds, he offers an exuberant commentary on each course. It reminds him of the time he dined at a famous restaurant in Paris, the head chef of which was a woman who "was considered the greatest culinary genius." She had the reputation for being able to "transform a dinner into a kind of love affair," he said. "Yes, a love affair that made no distinction between bodily and spiritual appetites."

Ah! There is that essential Christian principle of *incarnation*. We encounter spiritual mysteries not by rejecting the pleasures of the physical world, but by entering into these pleasures *in the right way*. Christian fasting is *not* rooted in suspicion of the physical world, the human body, or the pleasures of food. Christian fasting is meant to teach us how to feast in the right way. Only those who know how to *fast* properly know how to *feast* properly. As we learn the proper rhythm of fasting and feasting, the joys of the senses become not an occasion of sin, but an occasion of grace!

This is what happens through Babette's exotic feast. With Lorens leading the way, slowly but surely a taste of redemption makes its way around the table. As the people open themselves to this occasion of grace, the Lord works wonders in their *spirits* through the delight of their *senses*. Old wrongs are confessed. Old grievances are forgiven. Old loves are rekindled. And the people realize that this was not an "evil power" at work, but a divine one.

Later, the sisters learn that Babette had spent all of her winnings on the feast. To ease their concern, Babette confesses that she didn't spend all she had only for them: "Papin used to say,

'Throughout the world sounds one long cry from the heart of the artist: Give me the chance to do my very best.' " At this Filippa seems to realize that like the fearful servant in the Gospel parable she had buried her talent. Thanks to Babette's great gift, Filippa's heart is awakened and filled with hope in God's mercy. The movie ends with Filippa embracing Babette in gratitude and repeating Papin's words: "In paradise, you will be the truly great artist that our merciful Lord meant you to be. Oh, how you will delight all of the angels!"

## THE WAY TO HEAVEN IS THROUGH DESIRE

At the start of this chapter we contrasted the path of the *stoic*, the *addict*, and the *mystic*. In *Babette's Feast*, Martine and Filippa (as well as the whole congregation started by their father) represent the path of the stoic. Lorens, on the other hand, represents the path of the addict. In the end, everyone is changed by the extravagant artistry of Babette, who, along with Papin, represents the path of the mystic.

Such a change of heart does not come easily. Sometimes, in fact, as the movie rightly portrays, it can take a lifetime. But if we let life's difficult lessons teach us, "There comes a time," Lorens reflects, "when our eyes are opened. Focus and colors change and show the way to heaven."

What is this way to heaven? Desire. If we wish to enter the banquet that God has prepared for us, we must have the courage to plumb the depths of our desires and follow them *the whole way* to the other side of their truncated distortions, in order to re-discover their original, wild cry for God. Along the way of this journey, we must "pass through purifying fire," releasing all the things we cling to that are not God (our idols), so that we can live from within the passion of an unadulterated eros, surrendering wildly, freely, and completely to the Eros-Agape Love that shot us and the universe into being—and, at long last, feasting on the True Bread of Heaven, Life Divine . . .

> Forever in the heart there springs
> A hunger never touched by things
> And if unmet this inward need
> Goes prowling as incessant greed:
> We reach and reach for more and more
> While with each gain we still seem poor.
> We work to earn what can't be bought;
> Through prayer and faith it must be sought
>
> True Bread of Heaven, Life Divine,
> Eternal Manna, Holy Sign,
> Our need of you incites our quest,
> Your presence brings our search to rest;
> The hollow, hungry heart is filled
> And all its grasping motions stilled,
> Our quenchless thirst is satisfied,
> And every need and want supplied.

Let Christ be praised forevermore,
Who makes us rich when we are poor,
Who sees the tattered, begging soul
Beneath the cloak of class and role,
Who hears the heart's unspoken groan
And meets our need as if his own,
To whom all thirst and hunger yield,
The bread whose taste is truth revealed.[28]

# CHAPTER 5

# THE LIVING HOPE OF SATISFACTION

*But I still haven't found*
*What I'm lookin' for*

—U2[1]

I've already confessed that I'm a big U2 fan. Ever since I first heard their music when I was thirteen, I have felt like I've been on a journey with this band, and they with me. While the group was making their iconic album *The Joshua Tree*, U2's producer, Daniel Lanois, suggested to Bono that he write a gospel song. The result was the aching cry of "I Still Haven't Found What I'm Looking For," which Bono called "a gospel song for a restless spirit."[2]

Throughout the '80s, Christians who followed U2 were wondering if Bono and the boys were "true believers." Most of the band professed some form of belief in Christ, and their music was full of biblical imagery, but these guys were also secular rock stars who smoked, drank, and dropped occasional "f-bombs." In other words, they didn't fit in with the "church" crowd, which made their claim to faith dubious among said crowd.

When Bono sang in this "gospel song for a restless spirit" that he believed in Christ's redemptive work on the cross, but he still hadn't found what he was looking for, all suspicions were confirmed: Bono was *not* a "true believer." I mean, once you've found Christ, your search is over, right? You've arrived. No more questions need to be asked since "Jesus is the answer!" Your every desire is now fulfilled.

Really? I don't know about you, but I'm looking for an ecstasy and bliss that lasts forever. I'm looking for a union and an intimacy in which everyone and everything is reconciled in rapturous Love, in which every human heart is *on fire* with divine Love, divine joy, and divine peace. I'm looking for an eternal homeland in which evil is no more, all wrongs are set right, every injustice is addressed, all pain and sorrow and suffering are redeemed, and every tear is wiped from our eyes. I look around at the world we live in today, not to mention the junk that remains in my own heart, and it is abundantly clear that I still haven't found what I'm looking for.

If eros is meant to lead us to the infinite, then in this life we will be ever seeking and never satisfied.[3] That, I think, is what Bono was singing about. From that perspective his song of longing is not a statement of doubt and despondency, but a very realistic statement of faith and hope: for one would not continue the search if he had lost faith or given up hope.

## THE SEEKING

Caryll Houselander, an English artist and mystical writer of the mid-twentieth century, wrote: "If instead of using the expression 'spiritual life' we used 'the seeking,' we should set out from the beginning and go on to the end [of the journey] with a clearer idea of what our life with God will be on this earth; and we should be less vulnerable, that is to say, less easily shattered by disillusionment and discouragement."[4]

"Seek and you shall find" (Matt. 7:7). This is the essence of the journey, the essence of the so-called spiritual life. It is a constant ongoing search, driven by a mad desire and an unquenchable thirst that haunts us and never quits. Christianity does not supply ready-made answers to life's questions, and it certainly doesn't erase the yearning we feel inside. Rather it awakens that yearning and *increases* it . . . unto folly, unto "madness" . . . unto *infinity*. . . .

Among all the great mystic saints, Saint Thérèse of Lisieux wrote of this folly with particular expressiveness: "Ah! my Jesus, pardon me if I am unreasonable in wishing to express my desires and longings which reach even unto infinity. Pardon me and heal my soul by giving her what she longs for so much! . . . Jesus, Jesus, if I wanted to write all my desires, I would have to borrow Your *Book of Life*." Thérèse was afraid of being "overwhelmed under the weight of [her] bold desires" which were "*greater* than the universe" and caused in her "the greatest martyrdom." And yet she was convinced that God would not allow her to experience such bold desires "unless He wanted to grant them." "I am certain, then, that You will grant my desires; I know, O my God! that *the more You want to give, the more You make us desire.*" With such confidence in desire's satisfaction, "ardent thirst" itself, wrote Saint Thérèse, becomes "the most delightful drink of His love."[5]

And so "the seeking" itself, when we embark upon it wholeheartedly, offers a rich kind of satisfaction in this life. So long as we're on earth, we live in the tension of what theologians call the "already—but not yet" of redemption. The living bread has *already* come down from heaven, and we *already* have access to it here and now through the life of prayer and the sacraments, especially Holy Communion. But the sacramental life is *not yet* life in its final form; it's *not yet* the ultimate arrival. Christ "our Life" has already come to us, but he also tells us that it's for our own good that he "goes away" (see John 16:7).

"He goes away," Houselander observes, "that we may seek him. The sense of loss, the awareness of insufficiency, makes us long for him as he is; it makes us willing to go out from ourselves and find him where he is." That's why it's good for us that he "goes away." The emptiness we feel, the gnawing void "must be there that he may fill it; and we must be aware of it," says Houselander, "in order that we may want him to fill it."[6] That "wanting him to fill it" becomes our most ardent desire, our most ardent hope.

And it is that *living hope* that enables us to bear with the torments of our yearning in this life.

## SAVED IN HOPE

Hope is the "virtue by which we desire the kingdom of heaven and eternal life as our happiness, placing our trust in Christ's promises."[7] Hope, as a Christian virtue, redirects our desires toward that which alone can satisfy them, opening up our hearts in expectation of the eternal bliss for which we are created.[8] In other words, hope directs *desire* according to the divine *design* enabling us to reach our ultimate *destiny*.

In his Letter to the Romans, Paul speaks of hope as follows: "We know that the whole creation has been groaning as in the pains of childbirth right up to the present time. Not only so, but we ourselves . . . groan inwardly as we wait eagerly for . . . the redemption of our bodies. For in this hope we were saved" (Rom. 8:22–24).

Paul proclaims that hope in the "redemption of our bodies" is what *saves* us as Christians. As we said from the start, our bodies are not mere "shells" in which our souls dwell. We are incarnate spirits, spiritualized bodies. The redemption of our bodies is the redemption of our incarnate humanity. The redemption of the body is the hope of living a perfectly integrated life—body and soul. It is the hope of having every longing fulfilled and participating in the eternal wedding banquet. And it is precisely a living, trustworthy hope in this banquet that "saves" us in this life. But saves us from what? Hope in the banquet saves us from sin: first and foremost, the sin of despair. Let me explain.

When there is no hope of an eternal banquet that will satisfy our hunger, our hunger is only a cause for despair. That's what despair is: hopelessness. In turn, when there is no hope of an eternal banquet that will satisfy our hunger, we start grasping at the pleasures of this world in a disordered way. We take our desire for infinity to finite things and "miss the mark." Hope in the eternal banquet enables us to direct our desires *for* infinity *to* Infinity, thus saving us from "missing the mark," that is, saving us from *sin* (recall the Hebrew word for "sin" means "to miss the mark").

In his marvelous letter *Saved in Hope,* Benedict XVI wrote: "Redemption is offered to us in the sense that we have been given hope, trustworthy hope, by virtue of which we can face our present: the present, even if it is arduous, can be lived and accepted if it leads toward a goal, if we can be sure of this goal, and if the goal is great enough to justify the effort of the journey."[9]

Our quest for happiness puts us on a rugged mountain pass, with many obstacles, challenges, and dangers to overcome. Sometimes the journey can seem unbearable. "Is not man's life on earth a drudgery?" asks Job (Job 7:1). Sometimes it sure seems that way. When people ask me, "Are you happy?" I always want to say that it depends how you define the term. Augustine said that happiness is "having everything you want and wanting nothing wrongly."[10] If that's what's meant by the question, then my answer (so long as I'm on this earth) will be "not yet." We are pilgrims. This life offers many astounding glimmers of happiness, but not happiness itself—at least not happiness as defined by Augustine. But I do have *hope* in happiness. I do have *hope* that someday I will have everything I want and want nothing wrongly—which is to say I believe that someday my desire *for* infinity will be met *with* infinity, not in some ethereal way, but in a tangible, even bodily way. For in Jesus Christ, infinity has given itself over to us in a tangible, bodily way and has promised an unfathomable gift: human participation in *infinity*.

Somehow (how, we do not know) our human, bodily selves will one day be glorified, divinized, infinitized . . . *if*, that is, we have the courage to open eros to Eros. Moreover, not only will we *possess* infinity, we will *be possessed by* infinity; not only will we *have* the fire of Love we long for, we will *become* it—just as, to borrow Saint John of the Cross's image, the log that catches fire burns so hot that it *becomes the fire*.

This is the hope that Christ holds out to us. And I don't know about you, but if this is real, I want in!

How does one gain access? Faith. For faith, "in its deepest essence," wrote John Paul II, is "*the openness* of the human heart to the gift" . . . to the gift of infinite bliss that is God himself.[11] Lord, I *do* believe. Help my unbelief! If we enter into this hope, if we stake our life on it and place our faith in it, opening our hearts to it, we will indeed be "saved *in* hope" and "saved *by* hope." In turn, that hope of satisfying eros will, indeed, provide some real, tangible happiness in this life. For, when hope breaks through our fears and doubts, life is different. We have a true sense of purpose, direction, meaning. We have a destiny, an inheritance: "The measuring line has marked out a lovely place for me; my inheritance is my great delight" (Ps. 16:6).

Beyond the tears of sorrow and sadness that we shed in this life, hope brings tears of sweetness and joy. Hope may break through in a song, a sunset, a poem, a movie, an unexpected act of kindness, a good laugh, the birth of a child, the embrace of a loved one. And when these moments come (they can't really be manufactured, although we can dispose ourselves to them) we should drink them in . . . and listen. If we listen, we can almost hear a voice whispering to our hearts: "It is good to be here. Rest here for a while. Savor it. For this is a taste, a taste of what is to come. Let it lift you up. Let it *fire* you up. Let it give you hope. You're not crazy. You're not wrong to believe there's something more. You will not be unhappy. Have faith. Trust. Open to the gift. It's coming. Your desire for *Life* is not in vain."

## WE NEED HOPE SO WE DON'T FORGET

Good movies often instill a sense of hope in me, but none like *Shawshank Redemption*. The whole movie is about hope. The tagline on the poster reads: "Fear can hold you prisoner. Hope can set you free."

The story begins when Andy Dufresne (Tim Robbins) is sentenced to two life terms at Shawshank State Prison for a double murder he didn't commit. He becomes fast friends with fellow inmate Red (Morgan Freeman), who's serving a life sentence for a murder he did commit. As we let the story sink in, we realize that the prison serves as an allegory for this world, and various characters represent different human approaches to the shackles, burdens, and injustices of life.

The enemy of hope in this film is "institutionalization," the process by which inmates become so familiar with and dependent upon the routine of prison life that freedom—"life on the outside"—appears as a mirage, as it was for Red; or as a threat, as it was for another character named Brooks. Brooks was released on parole as an elderly man. But because he had spent the majority of his life behind bars, freedom was so disorienting and fearful, he ended up hanging himself in his halfway house apartment. The fate of Brooks shows us that a person can remain imprisoned even when he's free; on the other hand, Andy shows us that one can remain free even while imprisoned.

One of my favorite scenes—not only in this movie, but of any film ever—is when Andy, knowing full well it will cost him time in solitary confinement, locks himself in the warden's office and plays a piece from Mozart's *The Marriage of Figaro* over the PA system for everyone in the prison to hear. Hardened criminals stop in their tracks, pierced by beauty. Andy reclines in bliss at the warden's desk. And Red observes that "for the briefest of moments . . . every last man in Shawshank felt free."

As the scene continues, the enraged warden bangs on the door and yells through the glass at Andy to turn it off. Andy motions as if to follow the order, then pauses briefly to weigh a decision. Knowing full well he'll get even more time in the hole for what he's about to do, he looks the warden straight in the eye . . . and turns the volume up. I *love* that holy defiance, that willingness to suffer greatly for the sake of beauty.

The next scene we see is Andy returning to the lunch table after his time in solitary confinement. What follows provides the key to the whole movie, and maybe even the key to this book. When one of his buddies asks Andy if his little stunt was worth two weeks in the hole, Andy says it was the easiest time he ever did because Mozart kept him company. "That's the beauty of music," he says, "they can't get *that* from you." But his buddies don't understand. "Haven't you ever felt that way about music?" he asks. Red responds that he played a mean harmonica when he was younger, but it didn't make sense to keep it up when he came to prison. Andy insists: "Here's where it makes the *most* sense. You need it so you don't forget."

**RED:** Forget?

**ANDY:** Forget that, that there are places in the world that aren't made out of stone . . . that there's somethin' inside that they can't get to, that they can't touch, it's yours . . .

**RED:** What are you talkin-bout?

**ANDY:** (Pausing and peering in Red's eyes) Hope . . .

**RED:** (Befuddled) Hope? Let me tell you somethin' my friend—

hope is a *dangerous* thing. Hope can drive a man insane. It's got no use on the inside. You better get used to that idea.

**ANDY:** Like Brooks did?

(Spoiler alert: you're about to learn how the movie ends.) Later in the story, Andy acquires a gift for Red, something to help him "remember," something to restore his hope and lead him to freedom: a harmonica. In the story line, this is analogous to the gift Red had acquired for Andy years earlier, something that gave him hope and led him to freedom: a small rock hammer. Andy used it to carve chess pieces . . . and, little by little, over twenty years—unbeknownst to Red or anyone else—a hole through his cell wall through which he eventually escapes.

The movie ends with Andy and Red's joyful reunion on a beach in Mexico. Andy had once told Red about this beautiful place and how, one day, Red could find him there. After forty years in prison, Red is released on parole and sent to the same halfway house where Brooks hung himself. Haunted by that fate, he follows Andy's invitation, breaks his parole, and boards a bus bound for the Mexican border. The final words of the movie are Red saying "I hope." The harmonica had done its job.

What is your "harmonica"? I hope you make room in your life to play it. Often.

# CHAPTER 6

# EXPOSING AND STRETCHING OUR HEARTS

*Bound by wild desire*
*I fell into a ring of fire*
—JOHNNY CASH[1]

The wild desire that Johnny Cash is singing about is clearly for a woman. And yet, as we've been learning, what we experience as an urge toward union with another human being is, in fact, at its deepest level, a longing for something far greater than anything another human being has to offer. Eros is a longing for the infinite.

This is why John Paul II insisted that we mustn't conceive of sexual desire in human beings as a kind of base, animal drive. Human sexual desire *as God created it to be* is something profoundly dignified and noble. Sexual desire takes us to the meeting place within us between body and soul, between the physical and spiritual realms. It's both a spiritual and a physical power within us that provides "a certain direction in man's life implicit in his very nature. The sexual *urge* in this conception," wrote John Paul II, "is *a natural drive born in all human beings, a vector of aspiration* along which [our] whole existence develops and perfects itself from within."[2]

This is not a license from the pope to follow sexual desire "as is" wherever it leads. That's a recipe for disaster. Rather this is an invitation to learn how to redirect eros toward Eros. This is an invitation to recognize that the sexual realm in the divine plan is meant to be a bridge into the realm of mystical union with God. *This* is why the two become "one flesh": to reveal the "great mystery" of Christ's union with the Church (see Eph. 5:31–32).

## REDIRECTING DESIRE

But, really—how do we cross that bridge from the sexual realm to the mystical realm? How do we make the leap from the "wild desire" we might feel for another human being to being set on fire for God? I recently got an e-mail from someone who was wrestling with this question: "I'm a guy who loves his wife," he said. "I also love to watch the Victoria's Secret fashion show. And I work at a job that's stressful and demanding. How do I switch the focus of my life so that I long for God the way I long for my wife and for Alessandra Ambrósio? I mean, how can I even do that?"

I love his honesty. And that's *precisely* where we need to start:

by being honest with ourselves and honest with God about what really goes on inside of us and *refusing* to cover it over with a pious mask. So I suggested he take it up directly with God by praying something like this: "Lord, why am I so attracted to Alessandra Ambrósio? What *is* this fire she stirs in me? I give it entirely to you. Purify my desires and show me what I'm *really* looking for." And then I encouraged him to *listen*. God wants to speak to our hearts about these things. Seriously. He's not embarrassed. He doesn't blush. He knows exactly why he created us as sexual beings, and he knows exactly how to heal us of our wounds and disorders in this area. But we need to learn how to open our hearts to him, and we need to learn how to listen to what he is saying to us. As we listen carefully and prayerfully, we might have an important memory come to mind. We might hear a song. We might see an image in our mind's eye. We might "hear" a voice speaking to our hearts. Pay attention to those things. Write them down in a prayer journal.

One of the things God wants to show us is that behind all our misdirected desires and lusts there is a legitimate desire God put there and wants to satisfy. Uncovering that legitimate desire and entrusting its satisfaction entirely to God is critical to our healing and wholeness. As Father Jacques Philippe observes, "one passion can only be cured by another—a misplaced love by a greater love, wrong behavior by right behavior that makes provisions for the desire underlying the wrongdoing, recognizes the conscious or unconscious needs that seek fulfillment and . . . offers them legitimate satisfaction."[3] Some people call this "inner healing."

Allow me to share an example from my own life. I was six or seven years old the first time I was exposed to pornography. It went downhill from there. When I gave my life to Christ in my early twenties, I was in need of serious healing from all the distorted images that had been ingrained in my brain. One day I was being bombarded by flashbacks and I cried out to God for help. I heard a voice in my heart say, "Give all those lies to me and I will show you the truth you were really looking for." In my mind's eye I saw an image of a fire, and as I pulled all these pornographic images up and out of my heart and placed them into the fire, I prayed, "Lord, please untwist these lies and show me the truth." To my astonishment, what emerged from the fire, as the lies were consumed, was an image so beautiful, so holy, and so healing it moved me to tears: it was an image of the Christ child nursing at the breast of his mother. My heart cried out: "Yes, *that's* what I had been looking for the whole time—to be fed like the Christ child in this holy, beautiful way. Forgive me Lord for all the sinful ways I have acted out, not trusting that you desired to feed this deep hunger in my soul all along."

Would that that had been a "definitive healing" and the end of all of my disordered desires. Alas, the inner healing we need is part of a lifelong journey that takes us through various levels of painful, interior purifications. Step-by-step we learn to expose the real contents of our hearts to God and let him stretch our desires beyond the things of this world.

Scripture uses two very visceral images to describe what I'm talking about: "circumcision of the heart" (see Deut. 30:6; Rom. 2:25–29) and spiritual "labor pains" (see John 16:21–22; Rom. 8:22–24)—or perhaps in this case we could say "dilation of the heart." The masculine image is not intended only for men; nor is the feminine image intended only for women. "Circumcision of the heart" speaks of the need in both men *and* women to "cut away" whatever hides or covers the most intimate "anatomy of our hearts" and keeps our most intimate center from being exposed to God. "Dilation of the heart" speaks of the need in both men and women for our hearts to be stretched to their maximum capacity—to the point that they are large enough and open enough to receive and even "give birth to" infinity.

Circumcision and dilation; exposing and stretching our hearts—this is what's required of us as we venture along the way of redirecting our desires toward that which truly satisfies. Another name for this "way," this journey of both exposing and stretching our hearts, is simply the way of *prayer*.

## PRAYER AS DESIRE

"The Fathers of the Church say that prayer, properly understood, is nothing other than *becoming a longing for God*."[4] The life of prayer is already in us: if we reach into our deepest desires, we will discover our prayer. To "pray without ceasing," then, as the Apostle Paul admonishes us to do (1 Thess. 5:17), one must learn how to live within the painful "ache" of constant longing. As Saint Augustine put it, "Desire is your prayer; and if your desire is without ceasing, your prayer will also be without ceasing. The continuance of your longing is the continuance of your prayer."[5] It is "not with the noise of words" that God hears us, says Saint Teresa of Avila, "but with longing."[6]

This means prayer can be a messy affair, for longing on this side of original sin is often messy. It makes us suffer. And that suffering often makes us peeved. At God. Deep anger at God is a typical part of the fallen human condition. It's in us somewhere, and anyone who makes the journey of redirecting desire toward authentic satisfaction—that is, anyone who makes the journey of prayer—is bound to bump into this primordial pocket of pent-up pomposity.

Somewhere along the line people of faith can get the impression that merely discovering this anger within them makes them "bad Christians." So whenever it surfaces, rather than honestly facing it and working through it, we try to stuff it, ignore it, and put on a pious mask. We do this with all of our brokenness and sinfulness as human beings. We're afraid to look at how broken we really are, so we tend to pave over it and pretend it's not there.

True contemplative prayer, however, as the *Catechism of the Catholic Church* observes, is where we "let our masks fall." It's where we get real with God. It's where we get naked, allowing our hearts to be fully exposed (circumcised). Only then can we hand ourselves over to God as we truly are—the good, the bad, the beautiful, and the ugly—"as an offering to be purified and transformed."[7]

## PRAYER AS EXPOSING THE HEART

I remember a significant experience of having one of my "pious masks" fall off. It wasn't pretty, but from another perspective it was beautiful.

I was on a retreat several years ago in which I was blessed to have as my retreat master a holy, elderly monsignor (an honorary term given by the Catholic Church to distinguished priests) who had been a confessor and retreat master for Mother Teresa and whose own spiritual director had been Saint Pio of Pietrelcina (Padre Pio). In other words, this was a solid, trustworthy priest. The good monsignor told me how Mother Teresa in particular had taught him the connection between depth of desire and depth of prayer. In fact, he said he had never known anyone with a more ravenous hunger and desire than Mother Teresa.

Through various prayer assignments on the retreat, I was led deeper and deeper into the "ache" of my soul. The further I journeyed, the more I felt like I was entering an infinite abyss of unsatisfied and seemingly unsatisfiable yearning. Lots of memories from my life surfaced, most of them having to do with stuffing the pain of unsatisfied desire. As that pain presented itself, I was overwhelmed with a sense of feeling abandoned by God. I felt utterly helpless in my inability to satisfy my yearnings . . . and I became *enraged*.

The good monsignor had encouraged complete honesty in my journaling, so the pious masks that covered my anger fell and I let God have it. This is what I wrote in my journal, with a few choice words censored:

Same place I always arrive when I look honestly at my yearning—anger. I *hate* this! What's the *this* I hate? My utter dependence. Here I am, Lord. Come and get me. You bring me to this place of yearning and I can do nothing. So here. Here I am. I give you naked, helpless me as I am. [Then I let it out.] I #$@# hate this utterly dependent, helpless #$@#. I understand why people don't believe in you, Lord. I get it. I get why people choose to be atheists. I'm starved and alone and unloved and unwanted and agitated and I can't do a thing about it. And you can, but you make me wait. What the #$@# is that!? What kind of God are you? Why do you leave me just to suffer in my yearning with nothing to do but wait!!?? Are you ever going to show up, or am I just going to die of starvation? Aaaaarghhh!!

I swiftly went to confession convinced I had just terribly offended God with my rage, my "lack of faith," my "lack of trust," and a long list of other things for which I was readily condemning myself. When I sheepishly confessed to the monsignor what I had said to God, the first word out of his mouth was "Good . . ." Expecting the next word to be "confession," I was flabbergasted to hear him say "Good . . . *prayer.*" Our dialogue then went something like this:

**CW:** *What? What* did you just say?
**MONSIGNOR:** (with authority) That was a *good prayer.*
**CW:** Excuse me?

**MONSIGNOR:** That was a *good prayer.*

**CW:** What do you mean? I just chewed out God. How could that be a good prayer?

**MONSIGNOR:** Haven't you ever read Psalm 22?

**CW:** Refresh my memory.

**MONSIGNOR:** It's what Jesus prayed from the cross. It's a "prayer of agony" in which the psalmist basically "lets God have it" for abandoning him. Lots of psalms express the agony you were feeling, and the psalms are all *good prayers.* What you felt in your heart was a share in what Jesus felt in his heart on the cross. You expressed it in your way, and Jesus expressed it in his, but it's the same cry of the heart. In fact, what you experienced was Jesus *in you* crying out to the Father: "My God, my God, *why have you abandoned me!*" You're learning to pray the prayer of agony. And it's not a prayer of doubt. It's a prayer of faith. You wouldn't be screaming at God if you didn't believe in him. You wouldn't be screaming at God if you didn't think he could hear you and rescue you. Same with Christ on the cross. That's why I said *good prayer.*

The saintly monsignor then explained that the sins for which I really needed to repent were those of self-condemnation, self-blame, self-doubt, self-recrimination, and false piety. A skewed notion of piety in my head, he said, had made me think I was being "virtuous" in condemning myself for this honest prayer. This "virtue," in fact, was the real vice, he insisted. And this vice is often what holds people back from true prayer, from letting our masks fall and turning our hearts back to the Lord who loves us, from handing ourselves over to him as an offering to be purified and transformed.[8]

## GETTING NAKED BEFORE GOD

I share what happened on that retreat simply to provide a real-life example of the kind of "circumcision of the heart" that is required on the journey of prayer and desire. It's exemplified in the psalmist's cry: "All my longings lie open before you, O Lord; my groans are not hidden from you. My heart throbs" (Ps. 38:9–10). Exposing our hearts to God in this way teaches us humility. For it's pride that leads us to "hide" in the first place. It's a pattern that goes the whole way back to Eden: "I was afraid because I was naked; so I hid myself" (Gen. 3:10).

We *know* our sinfulness is ugly, and we *think* no one could possibly love us as we really are. So we "pretty ourselves up" in order to be loved and accepted, all the while rejecting who we truly are. We take on a false identity, hiding our true broken selves behind a great many masks. I know, for example, that, fearing to face my failures as a husband and father, I've hidden behind an inflated image of myself as a "good husband" and a "good father." I've hidden behind a busy and "successful" ministry— behind books and accolades and accomplishments. All so many fig leaves.

But the more we hide, the more we begin to wonder: If I'm

only loved when I'm wearing a mask, am I really loved? Can anyone really love me when all the masks are removed, when my ugliness is on display, when all the fig leaves are gone? We don't only want to be loved at "our best"; we want—in fact, we *need*—to be loved at our worst. We need to be loved in our nakedness: warts, blemishes, and all.

In the journey of prayer, we're seeking "nuptial union" with the Bridegroom, as the mystical tradition puts it.[9] And, to go with this image, if spouses want to unite, they need to take their clothes off. This may be a startling and perhaps even scandalous idea for some, but not if we understand the deep mystical sense in which the "one flesh" union of spouses images Christ's love for the Church. God wants to enter our hearts and have us enter into his in a way that is analogous to the intimacy of spouses. But we have to be willing to be completely "naked" before him. "According to the words of Sacred Scripture," John Paul II wrote, "God penetrates the creature, who is completely 'naked' before him."[10]

John Paul II also insisted that we have a duty to show the world "to what depths the relationship with Christ can lead." It is "a journey totally sustained by grace," he said, "which nonetheless demands an intense spiritual commitment and is no stranger to painful purifications ... But it leads, in various possible ways, to the ineffable joy experienced by the mystics as 'nuptial union.' "[11] The Lord longs, thirsts, pines to enter this union with us in the intimacy of our hearts, so he can show us that he loves us *as we really are.*

Always with a tender love for us (although it can feel violent at times), the Lord accomplishes this "exposure of our hearts" through painful trials that the mystical tradition calls "strippings," "denudings," or "dark nights." Father Jacques Philippe describes this phenomenon well in the following passage:

> The trials or "purifications" so frequently referred to by the mystics are there to destroy whatever is artificial in our character, so that our true being may emerge . . . The [dark] night of the soul could be called a series of impoverishments, sometimes violent ones, that strip believers of all possibility of relying on themselves. These trials are beneficial, because they lead us to locate our identity where it truly belongs . . . [They also deprive] us of any possibility of relying on [ourselves and] the good that we can do. God's mercy is all . . . Progressively, and in a way that parallels their terrible impoverishment, those who go through such trials while still hoping in the Lord, begin to realize the truth of something that up until then was only a pious expression: God loves us in an absolutely unconditional way, by virtue of himself, his mercy, and his infinite tenderness, by virtue of his Fatherhood towards us.[12]

His Fatherhood toward us is precisely the love, as we heard sung in *Babette's Feast*, that would "never give a stone to the child who begs for bread" (see Matt. 7:9). The Father "satisfies the thirsty and fills the hungry with good things" (Ps. 107:9), freely offering bread from heaven "endowed with all delights and conforming to every taste" (Wis. 16:20). But we must learn how to "wait upon the Lord."

"See how the farmer waits for the precious fruit of the earth, being patient with it until it receives the early and the late rains. You too must be patient. Make your hearts firm . . ." (James 5:7–8). "Wait for the Lord with courage; be stouthearted, and wait for the Lord" (Ps. 27:14). It's in this waiting that our desires are stre-e-e-e-e-e-e-etched. Oh! It's painful! Our prayer, our waiting, becomes a lifelong groan.

## PRAYER AS STRETCHING THE HEART

Drawing from Saint Augustine's definition of prayer as an exercise of desire, Benedict XVI writes: "Man was created for greatness—for God himself; he was created to be filled by God. But his heart is too small for the greatness to which it is destined. It must be stretched."[13] Augustine speaks of this "stretching" as follows:

> When you would fill a purse, knowing how large a present it is to hold, you stretch wide its cloth or leather: knowing how much you are to put in it, and seeing that the purse is small, you extend it to make more room. So by delaying [his gift] God strengthens our longing, through longing he expands our soul, and by expanding our soul he increases its capacity. So brethren, let us long, because we are to be filled . . . That is our

life, to be trained by longing; and our training through the holy
longing advances in the measure that our longings are detached
from the love of this world . . . Let us stretch ourselves out
towards him, that when he comes he may fill us full.[14]

Here "love of this world" refers to our idolatrous attach-
ment to created things. In short, to be "trained by longing"
means to learn how to take our longing *for* infinity *to* infinity,
and to settle for nothing less than infinity. In this continuous
"dilation of our hearts," our desire increases until we are convinced that there really and truly is *nothing* in this world that
can possibly satisfy it. Only then are we willing and able truly
to "let go" of our idols—those created things that we turn to as
God-substitutes.

This is how we learn what the saints call "detachment" from
the pleasures and riches of this world.[15] Detachment does *not*
mean we become cold or unfeeling toward the true gifts and pleasures this life has to offer. Remember, the goal is *not* stoicism. The
goal is mysticism. When we are properly "trained by longing,"
every pleasure in this life is like a teaser for heaven. True detachment affords the freedom to rejoice rightly in the good things of
this life without making idols of them.

And so, contrary to widespread belief and practice, if one is
idolatrously attached to the pleasures of this world, the solution
is not to turn the volume down on our desires, but to turn the volume *up*—way up. This may be surprising, even unsettling, but it
can't be otherwise. We must have "great confidence," Saint Teresa

of Avila tells us, "for it is necessary not to hold back one's desire."[16] And, as Saint Catherine of Siena says, "If you would make progress . . . you must be thirsty, because . . . those who are not thirsty will never persevere in their journey."[17] If we stop thirsting in this life, we have either repressed our desire or some idol is posing as our satisfaction, and the journey ceases.

"But these saints who talk about increasing desire are talking about desire for God," went an e-mail I once received from a person overwhelmed by lust. "I don't feel a desire for God when I'm being tempted by my desire to look at porn and masturbate. It sounds like you're saying I should increase a desire that I know is only going to get me in trouble."

Let me be clear: when I say we need to turn our desires up, I'm *not* saying we should fan the flame of our disordered desires. What I'm saying is that disordered desire—however it may manifest itself in our individual lives—is a *reduction* of the original *fullness* of desire with which God created us. When we find ourselves idolatrously attached to pornographic images, for example, we are experiencing this tragic reduction of eros. The ultimate solution to the problem, therefore, cannot lie in reducing eros even more than it already has been reduced, and much less in obliterating eros. Rather, as John Paul II says, we must come to "experience that fullness of 'eros,' which implies the upward impulse of the human spirit toward what is true, good, and beautiful, so that what is 'erotic' also becomes true, good, and beautiful."[18] Turning eros up—way up—means precisely this: rediscovering the lost fullness of eros as a desire for the infinite, as a desire for God.

This is a long and difficult journey, but it is one made possible by God's grace.

Think about it: if "the banquet"—infinite satisfaction of our desire in God—is real, then there's no need to *repress desire* as the "starvation-diet gospel" would have us do, and there's no need to *reduce desire* to addicting, finite pleasures as the "fast-food gospel" would have us do. Rather, if the banquet is real, we can and must learn how to *unleash desire* so God can fill us full. That's what the journey of prayer is all about. If it seems daunting, you're right: it is! You might simply begin by praying from your heart: *Lord, I recognize these twisted, lustful desires within me. Lead me on the journey of untwisting them so that I might come to experience the fullness of eros as a longing for you.* Or, another prayer you might pray is this one: *Lord, I desire you; increase my desire;* or this one: *Lord, into your hands I commend the satisfaction of my every desire.*

## AGONY AND ECSTASY

The journey of "stretching desire" is exemplified powerfully in the loving sighs of the bride in the Song of Songs. She is "sick with love" as her desire compels her to search without ceasing for her lover: "I sought him, but found him not; I called him, but he gave no answer. I will rise now and go about the city . . . I will seek him whom my heart loves" (Song 3:1–2). "I opened to my beloved, but my beloved had turned and gone. My heart failed me . . . I found him not; I called him but he gave no answer . . . I am sick with love" (Song 5:6, 8).

Commenting on this "agony" of the bride's unsatisfied yearning for the bridegroom, great saints like Augustine, Gregory, and Bernard tell us that Christ keeps his bride waiting to increase and *stretch her desire*. Desire is the faculty that not only pines after the divine gift, but also receives it when it is given, so the wider our desire, the more we are capable of receiving. Christ wants us to be as wide open to his gift as possible, stretched in our desire unto infinity, because that's what he has to offer us: the wild ecstasy of infinite bliss.

Like the bride in the Song of Songs, our search for this ecstasy will involve the agony of loss, but the agony itself is a prayer, as is the ecstasy to which it leads. And so the mystical tradition speaks both of the "prayer of agony" and the "prayer of ecstasy." And this simply means sharing in the sufferings of Christ so that we might also share in his infinite joy and glory. "All these sufferings are meant to increase one's desire to enjoy the Spouse," says Teresa of Avila. God "is enabling the soul through these afflictions and many others to have the courage to be joined with so great a Lord and to take him as its Spouse."[19] In short, God teaches us courage in the prayer of agony because we *need even more courage* to endure the prayer of ecstasy. We need even more courage to endure the prayer of ecstasy? Really? What kind of ecstasy, then, must God have in store for us? Whatever it is, the Apostle Paul says our sufferings are nothing compared to the glory that will be revealed in us (Rom. 8:18).

Until then, as Father Simon Tugwell expresses it: "The gift

which God makes of himself in this life is known chiefly in the increase of our desire for him. And that desire, being love, is infinite, and so stretches our mortal life to its limits. And that stretching is our most earnest joy, but it is also our most earnest suffering in this life. So those who hunger and thirst are, even now, truly blessed; but their blessedness is that of those who mourn."[20]

> Blessed are you who hunger now, for you will be satisfied.
> Blessed are you who mourn now, for you will laugh.
> (Luke 6:21)

## PART II

# DESIGN

*Design:* a particular plan, purpose, or intention indicated by the form and functionality of a thing. From the Latin *designare*: "to set apart for a specific purpose." From *de* ("out of" or "from") and *signare* ("to mark" or "to sign").

# CHAPTER 7

# OUR BODIES TELL THE STORY

*Your body is a wonderland*

—JOHN MAYER[1]

Several years ago a friend gave me a picture book called *Magic Eye: Beyond 3D*[2] that promised to enable the viewer to "see what is invisible." It was my first experience with stereograms—those amazing 3D images that look like a bunch of jumbled shapes and colors until you adjust your focus and gaze *into* them. At first it was frustrating. You really have to train your eyes to see in another way, to look *through* the two-dimensional surface. But once you do, all of a sudden the hidden image "pops" in 3D and you're *inside* it. Whoa! There it is! And you wonder how you didn't see it before, how it was right before your eyes but remained invisible.

Adjusting our focus to see *into* a stereogram is a great metaphor for what we're trying to do in this book. Recall that our goal is to learn how to live our lives in 3D: to learn how to aim our *desire* according to God's *design* so we can arrive at our eternal *destiny*. Our own lives, our own bodies as male and female, and the world all around us is like a stereogram. If we were to adjust our focus when we look at ourselves and the world, what hidden mysteries might "pop," what might we see that we didn't know we could see? We look at people and things all the time without seeing *into* them, and as a result we're often stuck in a very flat, 2D vision of existence.

## NATURE IS SINGING TO US

The intricate design of creation speaks of the intimate designs of the Creator: his plans, his purposes, and his invitation to men and women to enter into his own Mystery, his own Love and Life. All of creation tells the story, but, for the sake of example, have you ever taken Jesus up on his invitation to "consider how the wild flowers grow" (Luke 12:27)? What mystery might he be inviting us *into* here? I have a Catholic priest friend who's a bit of a botanist with a mystical flair. He absolutely *loves* flowers. I once asked him what the attraction was, and dumbfounded, he said, "Christopher, have you ever seen a flower?" "Of course I ha— No, no, no! I mean have you ever really *seeeen* a flower?" What follows is a window into the mystical view of creation he shared with me that day.

He first asked me to consider why people are so attracted

to flowers. Why do we love to see them, smell them, and display them everywhere, especially in our homes and our churches? Why do we like to give them to the people we love? Why does a bride carry them down a petal-strewn aisle on the way to meet her bridegroom? We may answer—because they're beautiful, of course. Yes, they are. But *why* are flowers so beautiful? What *is* a flower?

To put it plainly, as my mystical-botanist priest friend said, a flower is one of nature's most beautiful reproductive organs, opened before the loving heat of the sun, so that, to quote the Song of Songs, its fragrance might be "wafted abroad" (Song 4:16). And that luscious fragrance is "wafted abroad" for one purpose: to attract "lovers" (pollinators). Some plants rely on wind or gravity for pollination, but other plants require insects, hummingbirds, or even bats to carry the pollen—the equivalent of plant sperm—to the eggs of the female plants in order to produce fertile seeds. In turn, when those seeds fall into fertile soil, "the wild flowers grow."

The goal in all of nature is *life*! The rhythm of time—day and night, months and seasons—serves the purpose of *life*. Soil and air, sea and sky, rocks and hills, sunshine and rain—all serve the purpose of *life*. Every living thing in creation is designed to reproduce. Every plant, every tree, every shrub, every blade of grass tells the story of a seed that found purchase in fertile soil. Indeed nature's reproductive process is happening all around us all the time. Take a breath. Chances are you just inhaled some pollen, some plant's attempt to find a mate and reproduce. And in this context I can't help but think of that schmaltzy '70s tune:

> Love is in the air
> Everywhere I look around . . . [3]

Open your window and you might hear the mating cry of the crickets or the birds. Take a walk through the woods and you might hear the love serenade of a croaking tree frog. As Caryll Houselander marvels: "If you ever [saw] a little green tree frog and watched him puffing out with a pomposity worthy of a dragon before croaking, you must have guessed that there is a tender smile on our heavenly Father's face, that he likes us to laugh and he laughs with us; the frog will teach your *heart* more [about God] than all the books of theology in the world."[4] When we adjust our focus and open our hearts to it, all of nature becomes an astounding *theology* lesson. "For from the greatness and the beauty of created things their original author, by analogy, is seen" (Wis. 13:5).

If God is speaking to us through the natural world, then it's clear that one of his favorite subjects is mating and fertility, coupling and life-givingness. One has to be blind (or stuck in that flat, 2D vision of things) not to recognize this unending "song" of love and life everywhere. If what I'm saying sounds crazy, "ask the animals, and they will teach you, or the birds of the air and they will tell you; or speak to the earth and it will teach you, or let the fish of the sea inform you" (Job 12:7–8). Listen, and you will hear all of nature singing its own version of the Song of Songs, that biblical "ode to eros" that whispers the secrets of divine love. Yes, it's true: "*The hills are alive with the sound of music / With songs they have sung for a thousand years.*"[5]

And nature's song culminates in *us*—in the "theology" of our bodies. Our bodies tell the story of divine love. This story is written into the very design of our masculinity and femininity. But we may have to adjust our focus if we are to enter *into* it.

## COSMIC EROS

Let's continue with this reflection to see if the mystery "pops" a bit more for us. Have you ever wondered why almost every language (English being a glaring exception) attributes sexuality to things?[6] Trees, rocks, tables, chairs, ideas, feelings, and virtually everything else is either "masculine" or "feminine." Without giving it much thought, we typically assume this must be a projection of our own humanity onto the world. But could it be that in the deepest origins of language, men and women were rightly reading something akin to sexuality *out of* the design of the world rather than projecting their own experience *onto* or *into* it? Could it be that our sexuality—our cry for "completeness" in the "other"—is simply a human manifestation of something much larger, something as grand as the universe, something cosmic?

Philosopher Peter Kreeft writes:

> Did it ever occur to you that . . . human sexuality is derived from cosmic sexuality and not vice versa, that we are a local application of a universal principle? If not, please seriously

consider the idea now, for it is one of the oldest and most widely held ideas in our history, and one of the happiest. It is a happy idea because it puts humanity into a more human universe. We fit; we are not freaks. What we are, everything else is also, though in different ways and different degrees. We are, to use the medieval image, a microcosm, a little cosmos; the universe is the macrocosm, the same pattern written large ... [And this] means that sexuality goes all the way up and all the way down the cosmic ladder.[7]

John Paul II expresses this same idea when he states that the mystery of marriage—which he calls the "sacramental covenant of masculinity and femininity"—is inscribed not only in our humanity, but also in "the world" in so broad a way that somehow it "embraces the universe."[8]

At the smallest and largest levels, we witness a kind of cosmic "eros," an attraction of opposites written into the very design of the universe. Whether it is the attraction between protons and electrons or the gravitational pull between stars and planets, all of creation expresses a certain "yin and yang," as they say in Eastern philosophy. It's the code that God has written into the very order of things—the "divinity code," shall we say.

The heavens declare the glory of God, the skies proclaim his message; day after day and night after night they speak. There is no place where their voice is not heard; it reaches to the ends of the world (see Ps. 19:1–4). What are the heavens saying? God is a *lover*: a *Bridegroom*. And precisely as a *Bridegroom*, God is a creator: a *life-giver*. Creation tells *this* story. In fact, in the next verse of the psalm we read that the sun "is like a bridegroom coming forth from his chamber to run his course . . . nothing is hidden from its heat" (Ps. 19:5–6). In this imagery, the earth is the "bride" who, in receiving the heat of the sun, also becomes a "mother," bringing forth an abundance of life.

## THE ULTIMATE PURPOSE OF SEX

When we open our eyes to it we see that all of creation speaks of the mystery of marriage—of the attraction and union of creative difference. And creation's story culminates in *our* creative difference as male and female. As the crown of creation, man and woman tell God's story more vividly than the sun and the earth or the birds and the bees ever could.

"Haven't you read," Jesus asks, "that he who made them from the beginning made them male and female, and said, 'For this reason a man shall leave his father and mother and be joined to his wife, and the two shall become one flesh'?" (Matt. 19:4–5). For what reason? The Apostle Paul tells us the reason when he says that the joining of man and woman in one flesh "is a great mystery, and I mean in reference to Christ and the church" (Eph. 5:31–32).

John Paul II says that if we let the wealth of truth in this passage sink in, it will reveal to us in a particular way what it means to be human, and it will make our supreme calling and destiny clear.[9] For this passage, according to John Paul II, summarizes the central theme of biblical revelation, the main thing God wants us to know about who he is and who we are.[10] Here, in Ephesians 5, we learn that the purpose of the sexual difference and the call to union is not only to reproduce the human species, although that's an essential part of it. It's not only for the sake of human companionship, although that, too, is an essential part of it. The ultimate purpose of the sexual difference and the call to union is to signify the difference and call to union of the Creator and the creature, of Christ and his Church.

God is infinitely *other*, infinitely *different* from his creation. And yet this infinitely different Creator does not hold himself aloof. God wants to be *one* with his creation. God wants to *unite* with his creation. God wants to *marry* his creation. This is what the mystery of Jesus Christ—the mystery of God taking on flesh—is all about: the marriage of Creator and creature; the marriage of divinity and humanity. What an astounding view of God and his plan for the world and for us! But there's even more to it. Remember what we learned in second grade: "First comes love, then comes marriage, then comes the baby in the baby carriage"? What we didn't realize then was that we were actually reciting some profound theology. Not only does God love us, not only does he want to "marry" us, God wants to *fill us full* with his own divine life. This divine infilling "is nothing other than the heavenly Father by a divine seed, as it were, impregnating the soul," says Saint Bonaventure.[11]

Oh how we long for this infilling! It's the fulfillment of the creature's deepest "ache." If the collective cry of humanity is "fill these hearts!" that's because in the very design of our humanity we find "a womb-like emptiness," says Peter Kreeft, "crying out to be filled, impregnated by [our] divine lover."[12]

Perhaps now we can understand more clearly why the Apostle Paul called the one-flesh union a "great mystery" that refers to Christ and the Church. Perhaps now we can understand why John Paul II believes that Paul's teaching on this point provides a summary of the entire biblical message. Christ is the one who "left father and mother" to give up his body for his Bride, so that the Church might become "one body, one spirit" with him, as the priest says in the Church's liturgy. And that's where it all happens for us—in the liturgy, in the Church's most exalted prayer.

## THE SPOUSAL REALITY OF THE LITURGY

Do you know why the Church has traditionally prayed her liturgy toward the east? Precisely because of the spousal imagery of the sun coming forth in the sky "like a bridegroom." The sun's rising is (quite literally) what *orients* the Church's prayer, that is, the Church's longing. She is the Bride awaiting the coming of the Bridegroom. In the Christian mind, it's no coincidence that the day we gather for worship is *Sun*-day. Of course, this is in remembrance of Christ's resurrection, but, as Benedict XVI wrote in his pre-papal book *Spirit of the Liturgy*, "this date came to carry the same cosmic symbolism that also determined the Christian direction of prayer. The sun proclaims Christ. Cosmos and history together speak of him."[13]

The Church has always understood her liturgy as a cosmic event in which she gathers up the elements of the earth and gives voice to the cry of all of creation for completion in her Creator, for union with the divine Bridegroom. In her liturgy, the Church, speaking for all of creation, gives her "yes" to God's marriage proposal. She turns toward the sun and "opens her petals like a rose" sending forth "fragrance like frankincense" (Sir. 39:13–14). There she becomes the "garden of the Lord"—fertile soil that receives the "seed" come down from heaven that brings divine life to the world.

And this, of course, is why Christians have always revered Mary. She is the embodiment of the Church, the embodiment of all that nature proclaims. She is nature's glorified life-giving mystery. She has gone before us all as "the Bride" who allowed her heart's desire to be stretched to the point of being able (quite literally) to receive and even give birth to infinity. Thus, Mary is the model par excellence of what it means to *orient* human desire, to open eros to God. If prayer is nothing but becoming a longing for God, Mary is "the open vessel of longing, in which life becomes prayer and prayer becomes life."[14]

As we, like Mary, learn to become "open vessels of longing," we too, like Mary, can have expectant faith of being "filled-full." With eyes of faith, we can see this infilling taking place sacramentally at the apex of Christian liturgy: the representation of the Last Supper we call "Eucharist." The term comes from the Greek *eukharistia*, meaning "thanksgiving" or to "offer graciously" (*kharis* means "grace"). In the Eucharist, Christ offers his body graciously to us, and we offer ours graciously to him. And so, as Joseph Ratzinger wrote, in receiving Holy Communion "there is a person-to-person exchange, a coming of the one into the other. The living Lord gives himself to me, enters into me, and invites me to surrender myself to him."[15] And this Holy Communion, he says, "corresponds to the union of man and woman in marriage. Just as they become 'one flesh,' so in Communion, we all become 'one spirit,' one person, with Christ."[16]

The Eucharist, of course, is the re-presentation of what Christ did for us on the cross. What did he do? As Saint Augustine wrote, "Like a bridegroom Christ went forth from his chamber . . . He came to the marriage-bed of the cross, and there in mounting it, he consummated his marriage . . . and joined himself to [his Bride] forever."[17] John Paul II put it this way: "*The Eucharist* is . . . *the Sacrament of the Bridegroom and of the Bride.*" In the Eucharist "Christ is united with his 'body' as the bridegroom with the bride." In fact, through the Eucharist, Christ "wished to express the relationship between man and woman, between what is 'feminine' and what is 'masculine.' It is a relationship willed by God in both the mystery of creation and in the mystery of Redemption."[18]

We are all born into the world through the union of man

and woman: that's the mystery of our creation. And all who are baptized are "born again" into a new creation through the union of Christ and the Church: that's the mystery of our redemption. We can see that the mystery of our redemption builds on the mystery of our creation, "clothing itself," so to speak, in its form. And this means both our creation and our redemption are "spousal" or "nuptial" realities. One takes place through the bodies of man and woman in their intimate embrace, and the other takes place through Christ's body given up for us on the "marriage-bed" of the cross.

And this means our bodies are not only *bio*logical; they are also and even more so *theo*logical: they proclaim a "great mystery" that is spiritual and divine.

## ADJUSTING OUR FOCUS

The physical world—that which we can see with our eyes—is a sign of something we can't see with our eyes but often "sense" at deeper levels of our being. We cannot see the mystery of God. God is invisible. But since we are made in the image of God as male and female, our bodies are a sign of God's mystery in the world. To speak of the "design" of our bodies as male and female is precisely to speak of them from the perspective "of the sign" (*de-sign*).

Our bodies are designed to make visible what is invisible, the spiritual and the divine. Only the body is capable of making visible what is invisible, says John Paul II. God created our bodies in their masculinity and femininity precisely to "transfer" from heaven to earth "the mystery hidden from eternity in God."[19] In other words, God created us as sexual beings (male and female) to tell the story of his own life-giving love in the world, and to invite us to participate in that life-giving love *eternally*. This is the "code" written into the very design of our bodies, our deepest desires, and into the whole universe.

If this "code" is *everywhere*—even stamped in our own bodies—why don't we see it more clearly? Again, it's like those 3D stereograms: we have to adjust to a new way of seeing. Most of us view our bodies through the biological frame we were given in school. Thank God for all that modern biology has taught us about the human body! Who would want to live without the miracles of modern medicine? But, when we reduce our bodies to something *merely* biological, we lose sight of the 3D reality of God's design.

Do you remember Peter Gabriel's song "In Your Eyes"? He sings of how this woman's eyes reveal "*the light the heat*," and that in her eyes he sees "*the doorway to a thousand churches*."[20] Powerful! That is a man who is seeing in 3D! Now let's reduce what he sees to something merely biological. The song would go like this:

In your eyes, the cornea
In your eyes, the retina
In your eyes, I see the lines of a thousand bloodshot blood vessels.

Once when I changed the lyrics like this in class, a student of mine shouted: "Stop! You're ruining the song!" Precisely. That's what happens when we reduce the human body to something merely biological: we ruin the song. Along with all of creation, our bodies are meant to be singing God's love song, the Song of Songs. It's sin that causes us to sing out of tune with God's Song. The good news that we'll explore in the next few chapters is that Christ came into the world to restore God's love song in us. He came to restore all of creation to the purity of its origins.

# CHAPTER 8

# IN THE BEGINNING

*There is a design, an alignment, a cry of my heart to see*
*The beauty of love as it was made to be.*

—MUMFORD & SONS[1]

When putting a jigsaw puzzle together, we typically start with the corners and then the border. Once the border is in place, then it's much easier to fill in the center. Without the border to frame the puzzle, it's easy to become discouraged by what appear to be "random" puzzle pieces. My friend Mike Metzger of the Clapham Institute once used the following example[2] to demonstrate how important frames are if we are to make sense of reality's puzzle. This may seem like a head scratcher, but bear with me—there's a definite point to this. As you read the next paragraph ask yourself: *Is this comprehensible or meaningless?*

A newspaper is better than a magazine. A seashore is a better place than the street. At first it is better to run than to walk. You may have to try several times. It takes some skill, but it is easy to learn. Even young children can enjoy it. Birds seldom get too close. Rain, however, soaks in very fast. One needs lots of room. If there are no complications it can be very peaceful. A rock will serve as an anchor. If things break loose from it, however, you will not get a second chance.

Without any image or context to frame the sentences, this paragraph is simply nonsensical. There may be a few things here and there that hold at least a little meaning for you: perhaps you like the seashore or perhaps you've used a rock to anchor something. But, overall, without the frame, not only do we get lost but we also get quite frustrated, and we eventually give up trying to understand what's being said.

Christianity is the same way. Rarely in our "Christian upbringings" is Christianity properly framed for us. There may be a few things that hold some meaning for us, but overall without the proper frame we get lost and frustrated amidst what appear to be "meaningless" dogmas and doctrines, and eventually we're tempted to give up on it, especially, it seems, when it comes to the teachings on sexual matters.

But maybe Christian teaching—whether it be on sex, the Trinity, the Incarnation, the Virgin Mary, heaven and hell, or any other issue—hasn't made much sense to us because we haven't been given the right frame. *Kite.* Now read that "meaningless" paragraph again.

## THE CHRISTIAN FRAME

Throughout this book I have been suggesting that desire—and, more specifically, desire for nuptial union—is the frame that illuminates the Christian story most brilliantly. Just like the word "kite" made everything in the above paragraph "click," so too does the mystery of man and woman and their call to nuptial union make everything "click" in Christianity. This, in fact, is the actual frame given by the biblical narrative itself.

Think about it: the Bible begins and ends with marriages—the marriage of Adam and Eve is the high point of the creation story in Genesis, and the marriage of the New Adam and the New Eve, Christ and the Church, is the high point of the redemption story in the book of Revelation. Furthermore, did it ever dawn on you that the first human words spoken in the Bible, "This at last is bone of my bones and flesh of my flesh!" (Gen. 2:23), are words of the bridegroom's desire for his bride? And guess what the final human words spoken in the Bible are. They are the words of the Bride's desire for the coming of her Bridegroom: "The Spirit and the bride say 'Come!' . . . 'Come Lord Jesus' " (Rev. 22:17, 20).

The whole story of our salvation, the whole of biblical revelation, is framed by the desire of the bridegroom for union with the bride, and the desire of the Bride for union with the Bridegroom. Bring these two desires together to meet in the middle of the story and guess where we are. We're at the biblical ode to eros, the "sacred love" of the Song of Songs.

The Song of Songs is first and foremost a duet between passionate human lovers. But it is also, as countless saints attest, an image of the passionate love God has for us and we are meant to have for him. And this means desire for nuptial union originates not just with the human bridegroom in the garden of Eden, but with the divine Bridegroom in the garden of heaven. It is God's desire for union with us that brought the cosmos into being and us with it. We exist because God wants to make a gift of himself to us, because God wants to share his own infinite goodness and bliss with us. And *that bliss* is what we desire at our deepest level. *That* is the true object of every aspiration of eros.

Being a Christian, then, means learning how to direct eros toward that which truly satisfies: the "nuptial union" of Christ and the Church. In short, these heavenly nuptials are what we long for (*desire*); they're what we're created for (*design*); and they're what we're headed for (*destiny*). If Christianity is not framed as such—as God's passionate desire for union with us and our quest for the true satisfaction of eros in union with him—it eventually becomes incomprehensible and even meaningless. More than that, it can even morph into something destructive to our true humanity. Recall Lorenzo Albacete's remarkably forthright statement that religion "is either the reasonable quest for the satisfaction of all the original desires of the heart, or it is a dangerous, divisive, harmful waste of time."[3]

## ORIGINAL DESIRES

"Original desires" are desires that go back to our original design, back to the very "beginning" of our creation as male and female and the original call to "be fruitful and multiply," to become "one flesh." They are the desires for the love, intimacy, union, happiness, and fulfillment that define us as human beings. In other words, "original desires" refer to all the aspirations of eros in that original state of the human heart before sin.

Christian theology calls this original state the "state of original innocence." And even though we left that innocence behind with the dawn of sin, deep in our hearts we still experience a certain "echo" of that mysterious "beginning," a certain echo of our original design when eros was properly oriented.[4] According to John Paul II, the person who wants to follow Christ must come to *"rediscover the lost fullness of his humanity and want to regain it."*[5] That, in fact, is what redemption in Christ is all about. The very word "redemption" is rooted in the Latin word *redimere*, which means "to regain." Christ comes as the Bridegroom to reorient the desire of the Bride (all humanity) toward the true wedding feast.

Christ himself is the one who, in discussing God's plan for the sexual relationship, points his followers back to our "original desires." When the Pharisees questioned him about Moses allowing divorce, Jesus responded: "For your hardness of heart Moses allowed you to divorce your wives, but from the beginning it was not so" (Matt. 19:8). In other words, something has gone wrong with the human heart and its desires. Something is now "off" in the way we experience eros—"but in the beginning it was not so." Through a proper interpretation of the symbolic language of the book of Genesis,[6] we can approach a certain understanding of that mysterious "beginning" before desire veered off course.

Jesus calls this thing that is "off" in us "hardness of heart." At least that's the familiar translation. The more literal translation is "uncircumcision of heart."[7] As we discussed in Chapter 6, we need to "circumcise our hearts" if we are to venture along the way of redirecting our desires toward that which truly satisfies. And that means "cutting away" whatever keeps the most intimate "anatomy of our hearts" from being exposed and open to God.

In "the beginning" we know the hearts of man and woman were exposed both to God and to one another because of this key line: "The man and his wife were both naked and felt no shame" (Gen. 2:25). This speaks of much more than the mere sensory experience of seeing the other's naked body. It refers to an interior way of "seeing" that reaches and rejoices in the interior mystery of the other person's naked *heart* in and through the other person's naked *body*. In other words, nakedness without shame refers to an experience of perfect integration between body and soul: it means that seeing the other person's naked body *is* seeing the other person's naked soul.

In our broken world today we experience a profound rupture between body and soul. For instance, there is a lot of physical nakedness taking place in the "hook-up" culture, but we are often scared to death to uncover our souls, to uncover those intimate matters of the heart that expose us as persons. As one female college student puts it: "I hooked up with a guy on and off for a year, and I don't think we ever had a conversation. Like, really, it was just, like, 'See you later.' "[8] Is this healthy? Is this what we crave?

According to Saint Augustine, the deepest desire of our hearts is to *see* another and *be seen* by that other's loving look.[9] Do you remember the greeting of the Na'vi people in the movie *Avatar* (2009): "I see you"? This deep "seeing" of the other sums up well the experience of nakedness without shame. In short, nakedness without shame reveals that "in the beginning" human desire (eros) was aligned with the divine design: to love as God loves.

## THE SECOND DISCOVERY OF SEX

Tragically, this peacefully vulnerable exposure is the first thing that was lost when sin entered the picture: "Then the eyes of both were opened, and they knew that they were naked; and they sewed fig leaves together and made themselves aprons." And the man says, "I was afraid, because I was naked; and I hid myself" (Gen. 3:7, 10).

John Paul II calls this the "second" discovery of sex. And it differs *radically* from the first one.[10] In the first discovery of sex, eros was "inspired" or "in-breathed" with divine life and love, which is to say, eros expressed agape. This is why the first man and woman were naked without shame: eros expressed perfect love, without any taint of selfishness, and there is no fear in perfect love: "perfect love casts out all fear" (1 John 4:18).

Let's pause for a moment to let that sink in. God designed sexual desire "in the beginning" to be the very power to love in his image, that is to say, to be the very power to fulfill the essential meaning of our existence, which is to participate in the life and love of God. This means the call to love as God loves is written in the very design of our bodies as male and female. A man's body makes no sense by itself. A woman's body makes no sense by itself. But together as male and female our bodies reveal a "great mystery": they tell the story of infinite life-giving love. Or at least they're meant to tell that story.

God had warned the first man and woman that if they ate of the tree of the knowledge of good and evil, they would "expire"—they would "breathe-out" his life and love (see Gen. 2:17). Lured and enticed by their desire for satisfaction, they took the fruit and ate it. And from that moment on, their bodies began telling a very different story. From that moment on, human desire was misaligned with the divine design. As a result, the original story of freedom, love, and nakedness was warped into a story of enslavement, lust, and fig leaves.

There's an important point to tease out here in the midst of the tragedy. The instinct we experience to cover our bodies in our fallen world actually comes from a desire to protect the original truth and goodness of the body. We cover our bodies not because they're "bad" (that's a heresy). We cover our bodies precisely because they're so *good*, and we feel an instinctive need to protect the goodness of our bodies from the degradation of lust. Shame entered only when lust entered. Actually, it's not so much that lust "entered"—as if lust already existed somewhere and it finally landed upon them. Lust (self-centered and self-seeking erotic desire) was all that was left of eros when the human heart "expired" or "breathed-out" agape. Lust, then, is an empty shell, a tragic and terrible *reduction* of the fullness of love that is meant to be there and *was* there "in the beginning."

By pointing us back to our "original desires," Jesus wants to awaken hope in us, as Andy Dufresne wanted to do in *Shawshank Redemption*. Tragically, we've all become "institutionalized" in a prison of lust (disordered desire). And this is why we need the music of "the beginning" to resound in our hearts. Just as Andy carried Mozart within him, so too we carry the music of God's original designs deeply in our hearts. The music is imprinted there, like a primordial muscle memory. And just like the men in Shawshank State Prison, we need this music so that we "don't forget." Forget what? Forget that there are places in our hearts that aren't made of stone . . . that there are places in our hearts that long for love as it once was, places in our hearts that are capable of receiving that love and sharing it with others. We need to be reminded that freedom is possible, although seeking it will take every bit as much patience and effort as Andy exerted to carve little by little through the prison wall.

We are *not* who the pornified media tell us we are. We are *not* valuable only if we can attract and arouse another's lust. In fact, lust *de*values us by reducing us to the level of a thing to be used and discarded. Our true value, our true worth and dignity, comes from the fact that we have been chosen by Love and for Love, and that Love is an utterly gratuitous and free gift. We have been chosen to participate in infinite love, in love without measure, in ecstasy and bliss beyond imagining. This is what we desire. This is what we're designed and destined for. Somehow, we know it. And this Love is ours if we would only open to it and *receive* "the gift."

# CHAPTER 9

# TRUSTING GOD'S DESIGNS

*To fill these hearts full we reach and grab for more*
*But I've found we've been reaching for the killing floor*
—MIKE MANGIONE & THE UNION[1]

The desire for infinity that haunts our humanity makes us all beggars. No creature can satisfy his own desires. No creature can provide himself with the "living water" for which he thirsts. This places us all in a position of *radical dependence* upon the infinite One to grant us the gift of his own infinity. Will he? This is the "test of faith" that God placed before us when, according to the symbolism of biblical language, he asked our first parents not to eat from "the tree of the knowledge of good and evil."

What's going on here? Does God really have our best interests in mind, or is he holding out on us? As we will explore more closely in this chapter, this original commandment is an invitation to trust in God's designs: he *wants* to feed us; he *wants* to satisfy the deepest desires of our hearts. Do we believe he will?

## THE ORIGINAL TEMPTATION

It is certainly no coincidence that the symbolism surrounding original sin is that of *eating*. Eve's attraction to the fruit implies that she was *hungry*. As we've been exploring throughout this book, hunger is the basic human condition. According to the biblical story, Eve saw that the fruit of the tree "was good for food" and "a delight to the eyes" (Gen. 3:6). She was not mistaken in finding the fruit good and desirable. God had made this tree and placed it in the garden, and everything he made was "very good." Why, then, were they not to eat of it?

The serpent's incriminating insinuation enters right here: "Did God *really* say not to eat from that tree? Aren't you hungry? And doesn't that fruit look good? What kinda killjoy is this God of yours anyway? What kind of God would give you this gnawing hunger inside, dangle this delicious fruit right in front of your face, but forbid you to eat it?" In the disturbingly insightful movie *The Devil's Advocate* (1997), Al Pacino gives voice to Satan's proverbial pronouncement on God as follows:

> Let me give you a little inside information about God. God likes to watch. He's a prankster. Think about it. He gives man *instincts*. He gives you this extraordinary gift and then, what

does he do? I swear, for his own amusement, his own private, cosmic *gag-reel*, he sets the rules in opposition. It's the goof of all time: *look*, but don't touch; *touch*, but don't taste; *taste*, but don't swallow... *He's a sadist! He's an absent-tee landlord!* Worship *that?* NEVER![2]

But are we to conclude that God didn't ever want us to eat of this tree? God certainly wants us to have a "knowledge of good and evil." But he doesn't want us to *grasp at* that knowledge on our own terms, apart from him; that is, he doesn't want us to *invent* good and evil for ourselves. Thus, as the *Catechism of the Catholic Church* puts it: "The 'tree of the knowledge of good and evil' symbolically evokes the insurmountable limits that man, being a creature, must freely recognize and respect with trust."[3] Trust. That's the operative word here. With the first sin, man "let his trust in his Creator die in his heart."[4]

By asking us *not to take* the fruit, God was inviting us into a relationship of trust—trust that he would grant us as a gift from *his* hands the food we craved. In other words, he was inviting us to keep our hunger "open" before him, believing that he would grant us the desires of our hearts. If we had remained in that position of dependence before God, we could have fed "without fear of death on the delicious fruit of... the tree of the knowledge of good and evil," as Saint Louis de Montfort put it.[5] As we read in Psalm 81: "I, the Lord, am your God... Open wide your mouth and I will fill it... But my people did not heed my voice... So I

left them in their hardness of heart to follow their own designs"
(Ps. 81:10–12). That's pride at its root: we don't trust in God's designs, so we choose to follow our own.

"*There is only one temptation*," writes Lorenzo Albacete. "All
particular temptations are expressions of this one original or 'primordial' temptation. It is the temptation to believe that the fulfillment of the desires of the human heart depends entirely on us."[6]
This is the deception that humanity came to believe because of
the cunning of the serpent: God has no intention of providing for
the satisfaction of our hunger. Believing that, we have only two
choices: starve, or take satisfaction into our own hands. And if
those are the only two choices, I'm gonna take whatever I can get.

But what if you're doing the same and it ends up that *you're*
taking what *I* want or *I'm* taking what *you* want. When we live
within the deception that there is no divine "gift" in which we all
participate, that there is no satisfaction for our desires apart from
what we *take* for ourselves, then it's a dog-eat-dog world and only
conflict and chaos can reign. As I often say to myself when I see
my kids fighting over a toy they both want: *There, right before my
eyes, are the seeds of world war.*

## THE WAITING IS THE HARDEST PART

Sin always testifies to our yearning for satisfaction, but not accepting *the way* to that satisfaction: the way of complete dependence on God as our *Father*. Looking at the world with all its
bitter sorrows and sufferings, it's easy to wonder if God really

has a loving plan for our happiness and fulfillment. To call God "Father" with a sincere heart is to recognize him as the ultimate origin of every good gift and to rest in his benevolent providence, trusting unflinchingly—despite life's many sorrows and sufferings—that God does indeed have a perfect plan for our satisfaction. To call God "Father" is to believe wholeheartedly that, in due time, he will provide precisely that for which we ache. As the psalmist writes, "You give them their food at the proper time. You open your hand and satisfy the desires of every living thing" (Ps. 145:15–16).

It's that "due time" part that makes us particularly nervous. As Tom Petty put it, "The waiting is the hardest part."[7] Precisely in that waiting, we must "suffer the ache," continue to trust, and refuse to grasp at satisfaction. In other words, we must stay in our *poverty*. We must remain in the posture of the "open Bride" who awaits the coming of the Bridegroom with joyful expectation, and plenty of oil (faith) to keep her lamp afire. "Wait for the Lord with courage; be stouthearted, and wait for the Lord" (Ps. 27:14).

Let us recall that faith in its deepest essence is *the openness* of the human heart to God's gift.[8] Sin, in its deepest essence, is the opposite of faith. It is the closing of the heart to God's Fatherhood and a grasping at the gift of divine life he wishes to grant us. "*This is truly the key for interpreting reality,*" wrote John Paul II. "*Original sin is not only the violation of a positive command of God ... Original sin attempts, then, to abolish fatherhood, destroying its rays which permeate the created world, placing in doubt the truth about God who is Love and leaving man only with a sense of the master-slave relationship."* In turn, "man feels goaded to do battle against God [and] driven to take sides against the master who kept him enslaved."[9]

When we come to see God as a tyrant, the last thing we want to do is remain "receptive" before him. That makes us too vulnerable. We still want divine life (happiness, satisfaction), but *not* in such a way that we have to be dependent on God to give it to us.[10] We want it on *our* terms. We want to be "like God," but *without* God.[11] It's called "pride." Quoting lyrics once again from Mike Mangione & the Union:

> **Wrapped deep in pride we take what's never been denied**
> **And with each step we bandage our sides to the killing floor[12]**

With this dark image of pride leading to death, the song then lets light break through in a ray of hope: *"But we can sing Hallelujah."* What enables us to sing hallelujah when we are wrapped deep in pride and strapped down to "the killing floor"? As we'll see in the next chapter, God's response to our pride is not what we might expect.

# CHAPTER 10

# THE DESIGNS OF REDEMPTION

*Maybe redemption has stories to tell*
*Maybe forgiveness is right where you fell*
—SWITCHFOOT[1]

Christians typically present Christ's death on the cross as the "price" that had to be paid for humanity's sin. The wages of sin is death (see Rom. 6:23) and Christ paid that price for us. That is indeed an integral aspect of our redemption for which we should be eternally grateful. But the designs of redemption are more manifold than Christ's paying the debt of sin, as awesome as that truly is.

One of the most important reasons Christ "humbled himself unto death, even death on a cross" (Phil. 2:8) is to show us that God is not who we thought he was; he's not a tyrant who wants to dominate us and leave us to starve in our hunger. God is a loving Father who wants to *provide for* us, who wants to *feed* us, who wants to *satisfy* our hunger beyond our wildest imaginings—even when we've doubted him, put him to the test, and spoken against him:

> In their hearts they put God to the test by demanding the food they craved.
> They even spoke against God.
> They said: "Is it possible for God to prepare a table in the desert?"
> Yet he commanded the clouds above and opened the gates of heaven.
> He rained down manna for their food and gave them bread from heaven. (Ps. 78:15–24)

Christ is the true bread come down from heaven that satisfies our every desire (see John 6:32–51). And this same Christ is God's response to our pride. In Christ, man who made himself God encounters God who made himself man. Unrivalled self-importance and pride encounters unrivalled self-emptying and humility. Man, a mere speck in the universe, considered equality with God something at which to grasp. Whereas Christ, although he *was* God, did not consider equality with God something at which to grasp, but emptied himself and came as a servant (see Phil. 2:6–7); he came as the bread of life; he came to be *eaten as food*.

## INFINITY AS FOOD

Eating always involves death. To satisfy the belly of one life, another life has to be sacrificed. We tend to lose sight of the "sacrificial nature" of eating when we buy pre-butchered, bloodless chicken in nicely packaged plastic wrap, but it's a basic fact. And it's even true of fruits and vegetables: their life must be plucked or uprooted (that is, ended) to sustain other life.

But what kind of food could possibly satisfy our hunger for the infinite? Is it possible for infinity to become food? This is the full-bodied Christian proposal in a nutshell: infinity *has* become food for us in order to satisfy our hunger for the infinite. Bread has come down from heaven, and whoever eats this bread will live forever. This bread is Christ's flesh given for the life of the world (see John 6:51). Faith accepts what our senses cannot perceive: in the Eucharist, the infinite One has freely sacrificed himself as food for us. And in doing so, Christ has turned the logic of the food chain on its head.

The little guy always dies so the big guy can live. That's the logic of the food chain: big fish eat little fish, much to the little fish's chagrin. But in the Christ-event, *the* "Big Fish" freely dies in order to offer himself as food for us minnows. Right when the "Big Fish" shows up and we think we're about to be swallowed alive, the "Big Fish" says, "No! You have it all wrong. I want *you* to eat *me*. Truly, I desire to *feed* you, not *eat* you. Stop persisting in your unbelief. Believe and live. Open wide your mouth and I will fill it."

Christ's entire mission is to save us from the lie that the satisfaction of our fundamental hunger is up to us. And to what lengths he goes! "You don't believe in 'the gift' of God?" Christ asks. "This is my body *given for you*; this is my blood, *shed for you*." And his flesh is *real food*; his blood is *real drink* (see John 6:55). Christ comes as finest wheat to be "ground into flour" and "baked into bread" for us to eat unto satiation. He comes as the juiciest grapes to be crushed in the "winepress" so that we might drink his gift unto intoxication. "Whoever comes to me will never go hungry and whoever believes in me will never be thirsty" (John 6:35). That is Christ's promise.

"All you who are thirsty come . . . without paying and without cost, drink wine and milk! Why spend your money for what is not bread . . . for what fails to satisfy? Follow me and you shall . . . delight in rich fare" (Isa. 55:1–2).

## CHRIST'S REFUSAL TO GRASP

The more we treasure God's promise in our hearts, the less inclined we'll be to grasp at satisfaction apart from God and his plan for us. Like the psalmist, we'll be able to say: "I treasure your promise in my heart lest I sin against you" (Ps. 119:11). "Apart from you I want nothing on earth. My body and my heart faint for joy; God is my possession forever" (Ps. 73:25–26). This was the disposition of Christ, who saves us from our plight not only by becoming the bread and wine we desire, but also by "living through" the temptation to "grasp" at satisfaction without ever giving in to it, as Scripture says, he was "tempted as we are, but without sinning" (Heb. 4:15).

After fasting for forty days in the desert, Jesus was *hungry*. "You needn't be hungry any longer," went the temptation. "If you're the Son of God, feed yourself." Sounds familiar, doesn't it? The New Adam is here facing the same test that the first Adam faced. "If you're the Son of God, throw yourself down. God promised he'd provide for you, didn't he?" And finally, "I'll give you everything you want, if you worship me" (see Matt. 4:1–11).

We worship whatever we think will satisfy our "ache," our hunger, our yearning. The tempter is always trying to divert our *desire* away from God's *designs* in order to keep us from our *destiny*. In short, he says: "Here's what you want. God's not going to satisfy you. I am." He always promises to alleviate our *hunger, fear,* and *poverty* with *satisfaction, security,* and *supply*.

In the desert, and even more so on the cross, Christ stared human hunger, fear, and poverty in the face, felt it "to the depths," and refused to grasp at fulfillment apart from the Father's providence. In other words, he refused "relief" for his suffering. Temptation always offers relief from suffering: "If you are the Son of God, come down from that cross" (Matt. 27:40). If Christ had done so, he would have rejected his posture of "receptivity" before the Father, and the "second Adam" would have committed the sin of the "first Adam" all over again.

In this context it makes sense why suffering, as I once heard it said, means "continued receptivity." Christ "stayed in the ache" and maintained faith in "the gift." He accepted fully the abject poverty of the human condition and his complete and utter dependence on the Father amidst the worst imaginable onslaught of temptations to grasp at satisfaction and "relieve" his sufferings. "No," he said. "I will not deny my posture of receptivity before my Father. I will not grasp to feed my hunger. I know who my Father is, and my food is to do his will. I will trust. I will not put him to the test. I will not come down from this cross. I will worship him and him alone. For he is my inheritance and my cup; he alone will give me my reward. He will not be long in satisfying the desires of my heart. Father, into your hands I commend my spirit. Into your hands I commend the satisfaction of my desires."

## THE FATHER IS TRUSTWORTHY

John Paul II once wrote that if "the agony on the cross had not happened the truth that God is love would have been unfounded."[2] Christ's "prayer of agony"—"My God, my God, why have you abandoned me?" (Mark 15:34)—shows us that God is truly with us in our agony. If the Son of God is *right with us* when we feel abandoned by God—in our unsatisfied hunger, in our ache, in our suffering—then we are not abandoned by God in our hunger, in our ache, in our suffering. For Jesus is with us *right there.*

Christ's crucifixion—his "staying on the cross" and refusing to "come down"—demonstrates that he trusted the Father completely. He remained in his poverty and total dependence until the end. But what testimony do we have that Christ's trust was not in vain, that the Father was actually trustworthy?

On the first day of the week—also known as "the eighth day," the day of the new creation, and the day of the Sun—Christ left his grave clothes behind and came forth from the earth as a New Adam. According to the *Catechism of the Catholic Church*, "The empty tomb and the linen cloths lying there signify in themselves that by God's power Christ's body had escaped the bonds of death and corruption."[3]

Everything in the Christian faith hinges on the resurrection of Christ. Indeed, if Christ is not raised from the dead, the Christian faith is in vain (see 1 Cor. 15:17). If Christ is not raised from the dead, God is *not* to be trusted. If Christ is not raised from the dead, God has abandoned us in our desire for the fullness of life and it's up to us to do whatever we can to satisfy our hunger. This is why the Apostle Paul says, "If the dead are not raised, 'Let us eat and drink, for tomorrow we die' " (1 Cor. 15:32).

But if Christ *is* raised from the dead, this means our cry for the fullness of life amidst so much pain and agony *has* been answered. It means there is no hell we might pass through that Christ has not opened to life, to redemption. It means there is no such thing as a hopeless situation. It means there really is a banquet freely offered to us from above that can satisfy our hunger. In Christ's death and resurrection, the wheat has been ground, the grapes have been crushed, and heavenly bread and wine have issued forth. Infinite satisfaction in this heavenly wedding feast awaits us.

However, we must learn to realign our desire *for* this feast *toward* this feast. That's what sexual morality (and all morality), from the Christian perspective, is all about. And this is what we'll explore in Part III.

PART III

# DESTINY

***Destiny:*** one's ultimate point of arrival; one's end or fate. From the Latin *destinare*: "to make firm or establish"; in archery—"to aim at."

# CHAPTER II

# CHASTITY IS A PROMISE
# OF IMMORTALITY

*Am I only dreaming*
*Or is this burning an eternal flame?*
—THE BANGLES[1]

It's not a dream. The burning flame of eros speaks of our heart's longing for eternity. It speaks of our destiny. Indeed, eros has a trajectory, it puts us on a certain path, and—depending on where we aim it—it leads to one of two ultimate arrival points.

When I say *ultimate* arrival points, I mean where we arrive in the next life. To speak about *destiny*, then, is to speak about the reality of heaven and hell. Heaven, says the *Catechism of the Catholic Church,* "is the ultimate end and fulfillment of the deepest human longings, the state of supreme, definitive happiness." Hell, on the other hand, "is eternal separation from God, in whom alone man can possess the life and happiness for which he was created and for which he longs."[2]

Hell is certainly not a fun thing to think about, or write about for that matter. In the past, Christian teachers sometimes focused too much on the reality of hell as a motivator for morality and too little on God's love. Today it seems we often have the opposite problem since many people assert that if God really loves us, there couldn't possibly be a hell. It's very important to recognize that it's precisely *because* God really loves us that hell—definitive separation from God—is a real possibility.

If it's true that God wants to marry us, it's also true that the heavenly marriage is not going to be a shotgun wedding. God *proposes* this eternal marriage to each of us. He does not force us to say yes. Forcing us would contradict his love. In other words, precisely *because* God loves us, he respects our freedom to say no to his proposal. We have every reason to believe he will stop at nothing to win our freely given "yes," but—because of the real responsibility of our freedom—we must maintain that it is possible for us to choose eternal separation from God.

The point is this: God honors our desires. If in the end we cling to something less than God as the source of our satisfaction, then something less than God is what we shall have. The question here is not whether we desire "heaven," but what we desire *as* "heaven," as the fulfillment of our longing. We all desire some kind of "heaven," some kind of lasting fulfillment. Nothing can change that about us. But in the end, if we're not aiming our ultimate desire at *the* Ultimate, we miss the mark. And when the mark is heaven, that's something we really don't want to miss.

## MORALITY AND DESTINY

All questions of morality, then, are questions about how to align human *desire* with the divine *design* so we can reach our heavenly *destiny*. This is the proper context in which to understand the Christian sexual ethic. It's not a prudish list of prohibitions designed to keep us from having fun in this life; it's a call to realign our desires with authentic love so we can be truly happy both here and in the next life.

If we make it our goal to realign our erotic desires with the truth of love, our selfish instincts are sure to put up a fight, and that's where the virtue of chastity comes in. Chastity is the virtue that overcomes the selfish pull of lust within us and orients the wildness of eros toward the truth of infinite love. If eros is ultimately the desire within us that seeks God, then do you know what all the sexual confusion in the world and in our own hearts amounts to? It's the human desire for heaven *gone berserk*. Chastity is the virtue that "un-berserks" it. And this is why the *Catechism of the Catholic Church* boldly proclaims: "Chastity is a promise of immortality."[3]

Our bodies speak a language in sexual love that heralds our eternal destiny: God wants to marry us and fill us with eternal life, eternal happiness, eternal bliss. That's what the language of sexual love proclaims and ensures when it's spoken honestly.

Chaste love says: "I am here to safeguard your destiny—to work for it, to lay down my life to ensure that you reach ultimate happiness in infinite Love. From now on, in fact, our destinies are intertwined."

Without destiny, there's no such thing as morality; there's no such thing as right and wrong. Let me explain. Think what direction you would need to drive to get to the nearest park. If that park is your destiny and you drive in the opposite direction, a person could rightly say, "You're going the wrong way." But if you have no particular place to go, it doesn't matter at all which direction you drive. There is no right or wrong way to go.

Do you remember that hilarious scene in the movie *Planes, Trains, and Automobiles* (1987) when John Candy and Steve Martin are driving down the wrong side of the highway? A driver on the other side of the median strip is trying frantically to get their attention. Steve Martin rolls down his window and hears the other driver scream: *"You're going the wrong way!"* John Candy, oblivious to his own blunder, responds: "Oh, he's drunk. How would he know where we're going?" Only upon seeing the headlights of two eighteen-wheelers appear on the horizon does John Candy realize what the other driver was screaming about.

Aren't we the same way with the Church sometimes, especially when it comes to sex and marriage? In her teachings on sex and marriage, the Church—motivated by love and concern like the other driver in *Planes, Trains, and Automobiles*—is saying to the modern world: "You're going the wrong way!" But most of us are like John Candy, oblivious to our own blunders, and dismissive of any such warnings. After all, what can the Church possibly know about sex? "How does the Church know where we're going?"

But maybe the Church, just like that other driver, sees something we don't see, knows something we don't know. We don't have to wait until those headlights appear on the horizon. Maybe it's time right now for society and for us as individuals to take another look at what the Church *really* teaches about chastity. A lot of us may discover a very different reality than what we had ever imagined.[4]

## TO CAPTURE THE UNICORN

The towering arches in the nave of St. Peter's Basilica in Rome are adorned with dramatic marble statues that depict various virtues. Perhaps the most striking is the ornate statue of a beautiful bare-breasted woman (one breast is only thinly veiled and the other is fully exposed) who holds an open golden rose tenderly in her left hand and in her right grasps the horn of a wild golden unicorn (see page 186). What virtue is this? Chastity. Yes, this is the image that St. Peter's Basilica, the largest and most famous church in Christendom, holds out to the world as an invitation to ponder the meaning of rightly directed eros. So let's accept the invitation.

First of all, many of us have been formed by such distorted ideas of the female body that a statue of a bare-breasted woman appears not only as a puzzling image of sexual virtue, but as a direct contradiction of it. The medieval mind, however, was not contending with the same barrage of pornographic distortions we face today. Christian art of this period often portrayed the virtue of love (charity) through the tender image of a woman breast-feeding or even through the evocative image of a woman squeezing her breasts to express her milk—the offering of her nourishment representing the outpouring of her love. Both of these images of love/charity can be found among the sculptures in St. Peter's Basilica adorning the tombs of various popes.

Because of the intimate relationship between chastity and love, it is altogether fitting, when one properly understands and employs the symbolism, to portray the virtue of chastity with a woman whose breasts are reverently revealed. For it is chastity that heals us of the pornographic distortions and allows us to see this woman's breasts *rightly*—as an integral expression of a holy love.

Regarding the objects in her hands, the meaning of these symbols is, of course, open for interpretation. It doesn't take a leap of the imagination to recognize that the rose is a symbol that evokes the feminine mystery and the unicorn horn is a symbol that evokes the masculine mystery. Her outstretched hands seem to represent her desire to bring the masculine and feminine mysteries together in their proper, creative harmony. Indeed, the unicorn seems intent on reaching the rose, but he must be guided by the fair maiden if he is to honor the rose and not violate it.

Beyond being a highly developed symbol of the feminine mystery, the rose is also a symbol of love and beauty, and in this context we could even say it is a symbol of the beauty *of* love, of chaste love, of rightly directed eros. Authentic chastity enables us to discover the richly textured and multilayered beauty of love. It is the beauty of love's potency and strength, as symbolized by the unicorn, but it's also the beauty of something tender, even fragile, as symbolized by the rose. The maiden holds the rose gently, with an open hand, as if to indicate the delicacy required of chastity. One does not manhandle a flower.

The horn of the unicorn, on the other hand (quite literally in this statue), must be held firmly. It symbolically suggests a sense of power and danger. And yet legend has it that if this power is properly harnessed, it can become a "horn of salvation," a source of healing. In short, this is an animal that demands a great deal of respect: it can gore you or save your life depending on one's reverence for its power. We see this respect in the maiden's gaze—she does not tyrannize the unicorn, but directs its power rightly.

## DISCIPLINED WILDNESS

Before it took on a kind of "new age" aura in the modern world, the unicorn had a rich tradition as a Christian symbol. In Dr. Chris Lavers's book *The Natural History of Unicorns* we read that the unicorn "appears in Old Testament texts[5] and Greek and Roman natural histories; Christians adopted it as a symbol of Christ, the Middle Ages as a symbol of courtly love."[6] It's within this symbolic tradition that we find the interpretive key for this beautiful and evocative work of art in St. Peter's Basilica.

The unicorn evokes a sense of mystery, illusiveness, and wildness. Legend holds that only a pure maiden could capture and tame a unicorn. It is said that if a virgin encountered a unicorn, the ferocious, untamable, and uncatchable creature would simply approach, lay his head on the virgin's lap, and become docile to her. Based on this symbolism, the unicorn often appeared in medieval romantic literature as an indication of the lover's purity of intention. The lover approaches his beloved the way a unicorn approaches a maiden—to be "tamed." Yet that does not mean that the unicorn loses any of its vitality. The spirit of the unicorn is not "broken" or suppressed by chastity. Rather, the virtue of chastity channels the unicorn's potency into something healing, creative, and redemptive.

And so the maiden who has "captured the unicorn" evokes an image of eros that is properly *disciplined* but nonetheless *wild*. In fact, a properly disciplined eros is even *more wild* than its "frat house counterfeit." Recall the distinction we made previously (see Chapter 4) between horizontal and vertical wildness. As "wild" as the horizontal variety might get, it is of its very nature limited. It loses all order in its hopeless and frantic search for infinite bliss in the realm of finite pleasures. Vertical wildness, on the other hand, without losing order, loses measure because it launches us into infinity. Vertical wildness is a rocket that—through much struggle, discipline, and a radical openness to divine grace—has found its true target, adjusted its trajectory, and thus it can launch with all its firepower without fear of missing the mark.

This is what happens when we "capture the unicorn"—we share in its mystery and direct its wildness toward the good. And so this beautiful image of chastity in St. Peter's Basilica helps us recognize that the discipline required of chastity does not stifle or extinguish the fires of eros; it takes them up into the greatest Wildfire of all, the Fire of the divine life, the Fire of divine love. And this is what makes chastity a "promise of immortality" a promise of heaven.

## A "YES" TO LOVE

How often is chastity considered something entirely negative, even an enemy of love? Right at the moment we desire to express our "love," they say, chastity intervenes with its "no." Chastity certainly involves a "no"—but it is a "no" to *lust*, a "no" that is an absolute prerequisite for learning how to say "yes" to love.

*"Chastity can only be thought of in association with the virtue of love,"* wrote John Paul II. "Its function is to free love from the utilitarian attitude"—that attitude that treats others as objects to be used for our own gratification. With personal discipline and the help of divine grace, chastity enables us to control "those centers deep within the human being in which the utilitarian attitude is hatched and grows."[7]

The discipline required here is not something stifling or destructive; it's incredibly liberating and creative. It's like the discipline required of a professional athlete or musician: it enables us to reach our full potential. Anyone can pick up a violin and make meaningless noise, but it's grating to the soul. That's lust. But place that bow in the hands of a professional violinist and you will hear beauty that expands the soul and lifts you to the heavens. Behind that taste of heaven, however, as we well know, is a lifetime of discipline, sacrifice, and training. It's the same with chaste love. If we want to live and experience eros as a taste of heaven, it will require no less discipline and training than what is required of a professional musician.

It's only when we call lust love that we consider chastity the "enemy" of love. When we recognize the difference between lust and love, we see clearly that love is *impossible* without chastity, for chastity is the virtue that orients all of our sexual desires and emotions toward the truth of love. It is a great big "YES" to making beautiful, heavenly music. It's a great big "YES" to the true meaning and dignity of the human body and of human sexuality.

And this means that *everyone*, regardless of his or her state in life, is called to the virtue of chastity. How many of us have heard admonitions to remain chaste *until marriage*. This, of course, is to equate chastity with abstinence. If we remain here, we will end with a terribly stilted and dangerously misguided understanding of chastity, not to mention marriage. This misguided understanding of chastity is dangerous because it sets up a very legalistic paradigm of repression and indulgence without training us in the ways of self-mastery and self-giving. Be chaste *until marriage* translates: I need to "cage" the unicorn (eros) for now, but once I'm married I'm "allowed" to open the cage. If this is our approach to chastity, get ready to be gored.

Chastity is a virtue that manifests itself differently depending on one's state in life, but its essence is always the same: "Chastity means the successful integration of sexuality within the person and thus the inner unity of man in his bodily and spiritual being."[8] Everyone is called to this personal and sexual integration, regardless of one's particular state in life. In fact, this integration is essential to the freedom and happiness we desire as human beings. Chastity is "a training in human freedom. The alternative is clear: either man governs his passions and finds peace, or he lets himself be dominated by them and becomes unhappy."[9]

Our culture talks a big line about sexual freedom. But what does our culture mean by it? Do whatever you want, however you want, whenever you want, with whomever you want, without ever saying no. Does this promote freedom? Or does this promote addiction? If we are to direct eros along the trajectory that leads to heaven, we must be about the business of freeing our freedom from bondage to libido. This, says John Paul II, is the condition for living all of life together in the truth: freedom must be set free from the domination of lust.[10] This is the theme we'll explore in the next chapter.

# CHAPTER 12

# FREEING FREEDOM

*Freedom has a scent*
*Like the top of a new born baby's head*

—U2[1]

Much is at stake in the way we understand and exercise our freedom. "Freedom is the capacity for infinity," writes Lorenzo Albacete. "I am free each time I walk along the path that moves me to infinity." In other words, freedom, properly understood and exercised, is what enables me to reach my infinite destiny. However, as Albacete observes, "If I choose to act in a particular way that separates me from my infinite destiny, I lose something of my freedom and move closer to that abyss of not being free." I can be rescued from this abyss "only when the attraction of infinity wins over whatever is attracting me away from it. This is the redemption of my freedom."[2]

Let's put this in terms of the three "gospels" we've been discussing in this book. When the "fast-food gospel" attracts me away from God's design for my life, I'm heading toward the abyss of not being free. It may well be, however, that I'm confusing God's design with the "starvation diet." Indulging in fast food *is* more attractive than starving to death, but it's *not* more attractive than "the banquet." And this means the attraction of the banquet can win over my attraction to the fast food. This is the redemption of my freedom. This is setting freedom free to be itself and fulfill its purpose: to lead me to my infinite destiny.

## FREEDOM VERSUS LICENSE

I had the typical idea of freedom as a teenager: freedom meant doing whatever *I* wanted to do without anyone telling me otherwise. So I thought I was free when I tossed off the "oppressive shackles" of my Catholic upbringing in order to indulge my lusts. I'll never forget when I realized how un-free I was. At one point, having been bothered by a conscience I couldn't seem to suffocate, my girlfriend and I committed to giving up sex. I only lasted a few days. Freedom? No—that's called slavery; that's called addiction. I wasn't able to say no. I was confusing freedom with license.

Speaking to audiences around the world, I like to ask women the following question, and I always invite the men to pay close attention to their answer. I ask the women to raise their hands if they would like to be in a relationship with a man who cannot say no to his hormones. Never has a hand gone up. Women intuit (more readily than men, it seems, which is why I can't flip

the question and ask the men) that if we can't say no to our desires, our yes means nothing. If we can't say no, we're not free, and
if we're not free, we're not able to love. Sex in such a situation is
merely akin to what animals do when they're in heat.

Freedom is not liberty to indulge one's compulsions. That's
*license.* True freedom is liberation from the compulsion to indulge. Freedom is not liberty *to* sin. That's *license.* True freedom
is liberation *from* sin. Only to the degree that we are free from
the domination of libido are we able truly to become a "gift" to
another person, are we able truly to love. *That's* why no woman
wants to be in a relationship with a man who can't control his hormones; she knows such a man isn't free to love her. When it comes
to sex, such a man can only behave like an animal, or worse, like
a monster.

Doctor Octopus from *Spider-Man 2* (2004) comes to mind.
In this fantastical morality tale, he is the picture of what happens
when we abuse our freedom and lose control of our passions;
all hell breaks loose. And the first to suffer when Dr. Octavius
morphs into the monster "Doc Ock" is his wife. Earlier in the
movie he had shared with Peter Parker his heartfelt love for his
wife. Now, lured by the prospect of having "the power of the sun
in the palm of his hand," he has thrown caution to the wind during
an experiment with nuclear fusion, and the mechanical arms used
in his experiment have taken control of him. Amidst the mayhem,
his wife is the first to die.

Eventually, Doc Ock's unbridled passions send humanity

hurling toward the precipice on a train with no brakes. Only Spider-Man—here sacrificing himself cruciform—can save the day. In the end, however, Doc Ock himself must regain control of his passions to prevent humanity from being destroyed. The noble Dr. Octavius returns when he demands from the mechanical arms that have enslaved him: "You listen to *me* now." As he sacrifices himself to save others, his final words crown this story of self-mastery lost and self-mastery regained: "I will not die a monster."

The lesson learned in *Spider-Man 2*—a powerful confirmation of Christian teaching—is that being dominated by our passions leads to self-destruction and the destruction of others. Only by gaining mastery of the powerful forces within us that vie for dominance can we discover the truth that sets us free to love.

## WHERE THE SPIRIT IS THERE IS FREEDOM

In the language of the Apostle Paul, living in the freedom to love means living "by the Spirit"; whereas living in bondage to lust means living "by the flesh." To live "by the Spirit" does *not* mean we reject or negate the bodily aspect of our human nature, as is often mistakenly thought. Rather living "by the Spirit" means we open our whole body-soul personality to the indwelling of divine love: "God's love has been poured out in our hearts by the Holy Spirit, who has been given to us" (Rom. 5:5). By opening to that divine gift through faith, "that essential and *creative spiritual 'power' of love* reaches human hearts and, at the same time, human bodies."[3] And the more we open to this divine gift, the more free we become. For "where the Spirit of the Lord is, there is freedom" (2 Cor. 3:17).

A key indication of whether we are living by the love of "the Spirit" or by the lusts of "the flesh" is whether we experience God's law as an aid to our freedom or as a hindrance to it. As John Paul II wrote: "Those who live 'by the flesh' experience God's law as a burden, and indeed as . . . a restriction of their own freedom. On the other hand, those who are impelled by love . . . feel an interior urge . . . not to stop at the minimum demands of the Law, but to live them in their 'fullness.' This is a still uncertain and fragile journey as long as we are on earth, but it is one made possible by grace."[4]

The Apostle Paul writes that those who "are led by the Spirit . . . are not under the law" (Gal. 5:18). They're *free* from the law—not free to break it (that's *license*); they're free to fulfill it because they don't desire to break it. Christ didn't come into the world to shove laws down our throats. He came into the world to align the desires of our hearts with the divine design so we would no longer need the laws. The *Catechism of the Catholic Church* observes that Christ's teaching "does not add new external precepts, but proceeds to reform the heart, the root of human acts, where man chooses between the pure and the impure."[5]

It's only in as much as our hearts are rebelling against God's designs that we still "need" his law. To the degree that our hearts are in harmony with divine love, "his commandments are not burdensome" (1 John 5:3); they well up from within. Think about it: we are only bitter toward God's law when we desire to break it. Pick any of God's laws that you're bitter about. Here's a proposal: maybe the problem is not with God's law. Maybe, instead, the problem is just what Jesus said it was—our own hardness of heart (see Matt. 19:8). And maybe the solution is not to throw God's law out the window or constantly reinterpret it. Maybe the solution is to ask God to change our hearts. If today you hear his voice, harden not your hearts (see Ps. 95:7–8).

In our hardness of heart we see God and his law as the tyrant to resist when, in fact, the real tyrant is our disordered desires, the grip of sin. As I already shared, when I couldn't say no to my urges as a teenager, I thought the ticket to freedom was simply to disregard God's law. Only later in life, after inflicting much pain and suffering on myself and others, did I realize I wasn't being tyrannized by God's law; I was being tyrannized by my own disordered urges. It's precisely from those disordered urges that Christ wants to set us free: "It is for freedom that Christ has set us free; stand fast therefore, and do not submit again to a yoke of slavery" (Gal. 5:1).

## THE DRAMA OF FREEDOM

No one is as *free* as the person who sees what is true, good, and beautiful and desires it with all his heart. And no one is as *unfree* as the person who continually bucks "the truth that sets him free" to justify indulging his disordered urges. What a tragic irony:

such a person wants to be free *from freedom* so he can serve the tyrant of lust unhindered by what he considers God's "oppressive rules." How backward we have it!

God's designs are not opposed to freedom. They're opposed precisely to that which keeps us bound: license. How could God be opposed to freedom? He gave it to us. But what he gave us is the freedom to choose *between* good and evil, not to invent good and evil for ourselves. There is an objective order, a divine design, to which freedom is answerable. But today freedom has come to mean license to do whatever one chooses. "Choice," in fact, has come to mean "any choice is a good choice." Really? Does anybody even believe that?

Such a notion of choice is actually the *negation* of freedom. If any choice is a good choice, all choices are ultimately the same and no authentic "choice" exists—only whims, seductions, and addictions. It is precisely the objective order of God's design that makes "choice" something real, something dramatic.

This is the ultimate drama of freedom: freedom is the capacity for infinity. We yearn for infinite fulfillment, for infinite Love. That's our destiny, that's the "mark" we're aiming for. Freedom is the capacity to hit that mark or, through the abuse of freedom, to miss it. What should we do if we realize we have missed the mark and abused our freedom? Repent. And entrust ourselves to God's mercy.

The Latin word for mercy is *misericordia*. It means "a heart which gives itself to those in misery." We seem to think that our misery repulses God. But God is *rich in mercy*, and this means it is our misery that attracts his heart to us. Like a child who instinctively and compassionately wants to mend the wing of a bird that has fallen from its nest, Christ wants to heal us and restore us to our true humanity. He wants to set us free . . . free *from* lust and free *to* love. Distinguishing the two is the goal of our next chapter.

| LICENSE | FREEDOM |
|---|---|
| freedom to indulge compulsions | freedom from compulsion to indulge |
| negates love | affords love |
| do what *feels* good | do what *is* good |
| freedom *to* sin | freedom *from* sin |
| sees *God* as the tyrant | sees *sin* as the tyrant |
| God's law feels imposed | God's law is written on the heart |
| breaks the law | fulfills the law |
| any choice is a good choice | choice between good and evil |

# CHAPTER 13

# LOVING LOVE

*Is this a lasting treasure*
*Or just a moment's pleasure?*
—THE SHIRELLES[1]

Benedict XVI summarizes well where this book has taken us so far and where we still need to go when he writes that "love promises infinity, eternity—a reality far greater and totally other than our everyday existence. Yet we have also seen that the way to attain this goal is not simply by submitting to instinct. Purification and growth in maturity are called for; and these also pass through the path of renunciation. Far from rejecting or 'poisoning' *eros*, they heal it and restore its true grandeur."[2]

Without this healing and restoration, eros "is not an 'ascent' in ecstasy toward the Divine, but a fall, a degradation of man."[3]

Without this healing and restoration, we pursue happiness in erotic love, but we find heartache. We seek to be lifted up but are pulled down. Salvation in Christ reaches us *right here*—in our pain, in our disillusionment, in our broken hearts, and, yes, in our erotic yearnings. As Father Raniero Cantalamessa affirms, Christ has "come to 'save' the world, beginning with eros, which is the dominant force."[4] This is a dramatic and important assertion: the work of salvation begins with eros because eros is the dominant force. And the salvation of eros has one final purpose: to reorient us toward our heavenly destiny and enable us to attain it.

## BRING ON THE WINE

We see Christ beginning his work of salvation with eros at his first miracle. He comes to a wedding feast in Cana where the couple has run out of wine. What is the symbolism here? John Paul II observes that the lack of wine can be interpreted as an allusion to the lack of love that threatens the relationship between man and woman.[5] Since the dawn of sin, eros has been cut off from agape (divine sacrificial love). Or, to go with the symbolism of Cana, eros has run out of "God's wine." Christ's first miracle is to restore the wine to eros in superabundance.

Superabundance is an understatement: the six water jars that were filled to the brim held twenty to thirty gallons each (see John 2:6). Average it out and that's 150 gallons of "the best wine"—about 750 bottles. Oh the extravagance of the salvation Jesus pours out on us! And he wants us to drink up! Indeed, the goal of the Christian life from this perspective is to get utterly plastered on God's wine. Do you remember that on the day of Pentecost, when the love of God descended upon the apostles, some among the crowd accused them of being drunk (see Acts 2:13–15)? Yep, they were drunk on God's "delicious and strong wine," as Saint Thérèse of Lisieux describes it.[6] "Let anyone who is thirsty come to me and drink!" (John 7:37).

We should certainly rejoice in this delicious and strong wine, but before we get too giddy let us keep in mind that this wine, which is an allusion to the Eucharist, is poured out for us through Christ's suffering and death. The agony and the ecstasy, Good Friday and Easter Sunday, go together in the Christian life. And this means that authentic love always involves the cross. Love makes demands on us—radical demands. It's easy to resent those demands, especially when lust promises the same fulfillment without those demands. It's precisely here, in the lure we feel toward satisfying desire without accepting love's demands, that we must take our stand in choosing to love love—which is to say, in choosing to embrace the cross.

I remember, for example, during a time when both my wife and I were feeling the radical demands of love, how easy it was to catch myself dreaming about an "easier life"—with another woman, not being married at all, you name it. The temptation was to escape, to "come down from my cross." Jesus experienced the same temptation, and he remained bound to that harsh tree unto death. In doing so, he exercised a remarkable freedom:

"No one takes my life from me, I lay it down of my own accord" (John 10:18).

## LOVE VERSUS USE

We can see in Christ's free gift of love that loving love and freeing freedom are closely related. Freedom exists for the sake of love. Indeed, we're not meant to "store up" freedom for ourselves. We're meant to "spend" our freedom on love. But to the degree that we're enslaved by lust, we have no freedom to spend on love. We must free our freedom precisely so we can spend it on love. And only if we truly love love will we have the necessary motivation to endure the exacting work of freeing freedom. If we love lust instead of loving love, then we will see no need to free freedom from lust. We will simply indulge in our lusts and call it love.

It's certainly true that love and lust can sometimes be difficult to distinguish. A man, for example, upon recognizing a woman's beauty might wonder where the line is between treating her as an object for his own gratification and properly admiring her beauty as a person. But this question only arises among those who love love. Those who love lust aren't even aware of the need to make such distinctions. Lust holds sway in their hearts and they just go with it.

What we often call "love" in the sexual relationship, if we're honest enough to look at it plainly, amounts to little more than two people using each other. Lust impels people very powerfully toward physical intimacy. But if such "intimacy" grows out of nothing more than a selfish desire for physical and/or emotional gratification, it's not love; it's the opposite of love.[7] For the opposite of love in this case is not hatred, it's *use*. As our own painful experience confirms, to *use* a person as a means to an end or to be used in this way is contrary to the very nature and meaning of love. And it hurts.

I'm going back almost thirty years here, but I can remember very clearly the first time I felt used by a girl. I was in eighth grade, and a girl I liked "made out with me," so she said afterward, just to have a story to tell her friends. I felt cheap. Disposable. And I remember resolving in my pain: *Fine, if this is how it works, I'll just harden my heart and play the game so I don't get hurt again.* Truth be told, I can also see how I was using her, and maybe her dismissal of what happened between us was her way of defending her own wounded heart. Regardless, it set me on path of using and being used, and calling it "love." It wasn't until my college years that I started facing up to what I was doing and how it was harming me and others. The emotional wreckage I witnessed in the promiscuity of college dorm life made me start asking some big questions, like *What is love anyway?*

## WHAT IS LOVE?

Society says a lot about love and "falling in love," but what does falling in love mean? Is love something we merely *fall* into? What role does the will play? Is love a feeling? A sensual attraction? An emotion? A decision? What is the proper relationship between desiring my own fulfillment and working for the good of the other? These are some of the questions that John Paul II explored in great length in his pre-papal book *Love and Responsibility*.

There we learn that emotions, feelings, and sensual attraction constitute only the "raw material" of love. There exists a misguided tendency to consider them the finished form of love.[8] I might find myself attracted emotionally or physically to any number of people I encounter. Should I tell my wife I have "fallen in love with another woman" just because I felt a certain attraction to someone?

It's obvious that emotions and attractions are fickle and can be misguided. We need to engage our will in order to gather up this "raw material" and build something with it worthy of the name love. For we cannot properly give the name love to something that is only a particular element of love. In fact, these various elements of love, "if they are not held together by the correct gravitational pull, may add up not to love, but to its direct opposite."[9] This correct gravitational pull is found in the proper balance between love understood as desire for one's own good and love understood as benevolence in desiring and working for the good of the other.

As we observed at the start of this book, the yearning of eros reveals that we are incomplete, that we are in search of another to make sense of ourselves, to complete us, to "fill-full" what we lack. This is expressed in the well-known passage from Genesis:

"It is not good for the man to be alone" (Gen. 2:18)—and this is man in the generic sense, all of us, not just the male. If it is *not* good for a person to be alone, then it *is* good for us to seek the completion of our humanity in an "other." This is part of the very nature of eros. Love understood as *desire* recognizes the other as a good and desires that other because that person is good for me, that person completes me. In this way, that person and the love we share become a sign of our ultimate destiny: union with God forever, completion in God forever.

But love as desire is not the whole essence of authentic love between persons. It's not enough to long for a person as a good for oneself. One must also, and above all, long for the other person's good.[10] If one's love is *only* about fulfilling oneself, then we end up not with love, but with egoism. If one is not committed to sacrificing oneself for the other's true good, then love as desire degenerates into love as *use*, which is not love at all.

## BENEVOLENCE

Selfless desire for the other's true good is called benevolence in love. If love as desire says, "I long for you *as* a good," love as benevolence says, "I long for *your* good," and "I long for that which is good for you." Love as desire is not itself a problem or a defect; it is merely incomplete. It must be balanced out with love as benevolence. The person who truly loves longs not only for his or her own good, but for the other person's good, and he does so with no ulterior motive, no selfish consideration. This is the purest form of love, and it brings the greatest fulfillment.[11]

I remember the day I knew Wendy would be my wife. It was the day I realized she loved me with this kind of disinterested benevolence. Sad to say, such a love was foreign to me at the time. It caught me so off guard that I could barely believe it was real.

Wendy and I were part of the same group of friends in our college years. I had no idea, however, that over the course of about three years she was hoping and praying that one day I would be her husband. My obliviousness to Wendy's interest in me was due in part to the fact that during those same years I was interested in another person in the group, a girl named Laura. Various external factors (mainly Laura's father) had kept Laura and me from ever dating officially, and the whole tangled affair had caused me a lot of pain.

As Wendy and I grew closer, she once asked me why Laura and I had never dated. I, for my part, was very reluctant to say anything, because I had just learned how interested Wendy had been in me during the whole time I was interested in Laura. I was certain—based on my experience with other women—that sharing the story with Wendy would only make her insecure, jealous, and upset. But she seemed so sincere in her desire to know about it that I ended up sharing the whole painful saga.

Sure enough, she got all teary and emotional. *I knew it! I knew it!* I thought to myself. *I never should have told her!* Then, to my utter astonishment, as Wendy opened up to me, I realized that her tears were *for me*—that she was feeling *my* pain. She went on to tell me that for some time she had known that something was preventing Laura and me from dating, so she had been praying that whatever the obstacle was it would be removed and Laura and I would be able to pursue a relationship.

I couldn't believe my ears. "*What!?* Excuse me ... Run that by me again ... You're telling me that you were hoping to marry me all that time, but when you found out Laura and I wanted to be together but couldn't be, you started praying that Laura and I would get together?!"

"Yes," she said. "Wasn't that what you wanted?" she asked.

"Yes," I said, "but why did *you* want that for me?"

"Because love means you lay down your life and your own desires for the good of the other," she said.

I had never experienced such a selfless love from a woman who was romantically interested in me. I was utterly flabbergasted. And I knew then I would *never* let this woman go.

## LOVE MUST REACH THE VALUE OF THE PERSON

Once again, let's acknowledge that erotic love is without a doubt a search for completion in the other. But as love matures, it becomes more and more an unqualified benevolence—a desire to uphold the good of the other and work for the good of the other, even at great cost to oneself. As love matures, we focus less on how the other person *makes me feel* and more on the unrepeatable value and dignity of the other person. And this is a love for the other person as he or she really is, not as the person of our imagination, not as the person we *wish* him or her to be, but the real person—warts and all.

"The strength of such a love emerges most clearly," John Paul II tells us, "when the beloved person stumbles, when his or her weaknesses or even sins come into the open. One who truly loves does not then withdraw his love, but loves all the more, loves in full consciousness of the other's shortcomings and faults . . . For the person as such never loses its essential value."[12]

However, when love is based only on the pleasure and "good feelings" the other person can give me, that "love" will last only as long as those good feelings. When the other person's faults, shortcomings, and sins are revealed—which inevitably happens and inevitably causes me to suffer—the shoddy foundation of our love is also revealed, and the illusion of love bursts like a bubble.[13] Only when love reaches the value of the person, which is inexhaustible, does it have a foundation that lasts forever.

The Italian author Rocco Buttiglione put it this way: "Only the value of the person can sustain a stable relationship. The other values of sexuality are wasted away by time and are exposed to the danger of disillusion. But this is not the case for the value of the person," he observes, "which is stable and in some way infinite. When love develops and reaches the person, then it is forever."[14] And when love is forever, we're experiencing a human love that truly points us to our divine destiny.

Mature love is attracted not just by the sexual attributes or qualities of a person that light a "spark" in me. Attraction to such qualities can form the "raw material" of love, but if love stops merely at a person's pleasing and attractive qualities (sexual or otherwise), a permanent shadow is cast over the permanency of the relationship. Why? Because a person's qualities change with time. Furthermore, qualities are *repeatable*—attractive qualities can always be found in others and to a "more pleasing" degree. Individual persons, however, are *unrepeatable*—they can never be compared to, measured by, or replaced by another.

Love that hankers after what is merely pleasing and *repeatable* in a person will do just that: repeat itself with whoever possesses those pleasing qualities. In this case, the inherent "adventurousness" of love—the desire for expansion, growth, and new discoveries—will lead a person to take his delight in wandering from person to person. On the other hand, love that reaches the *unrepeatable* mystery of the other person is a love that's truly that: unrepeatable, stable, sure. It's an inexhaustible treasure that can't possibly be found elsewhere. In this case, love's inherent adventurousness finds its delight not in wandering from person to person, but from wandering ever more deeply into the heart of the one and only beloved.

Let's face it: life continually offers equally or more seductive possibilities of new sexual relationships—especially in today's world. If the person I "love" is only an instrument for my own pleasure, then he or she can easily be replaced, and the inevitable result is an atmosphere of fear and anxiety in the relationship: *Am I truly loved? Will I be abandoned for another?* The case is different when love reaches the value of the other person. Then the other is loved not merely for the pleasing qualities that he or she has (and which one can lose or which others could have in a higher degree) but for his or her *own sake*, for his or her true and unrepeatable value as a *person*. Only then is the sexual relationship something more than selfishness. Only then is the sexual relationship based on something stable and lasting.[15]

When love stops at a person's "pleasing repeatables," it's a case of the raw material of love failing to take shape in its finished form. Not that love is ever "finished," but stopping at the "pleasing repeatables" stunts love's growth at the very start of what should be embraced as an ongoing process of growth and maturation. And when love's growth is stunted, eros degenerates quickly into egoism and lust.

The person who is the object of such lust gradually realizes the sentiment of the other person: "You don't love *me*. You don't desire *me*. You desire only a means of gratification." Far from feeling loved and affirmed as a unique and unrepeatable person, those objectified by lust feel used and debased as a replaceable commodity, and they live under the constant fear of one day being discarded for someone more "pleasing."

## WE WANT TO BE LOVED, NOT TOYED WITH

Don't we long to be loved *as we are*, for *who we really are*, and not just for whatever it is we have that may "please" someone else? Don't we know deep in our hearts that we are never meant to be compared to another, measured against another, or replaced by someone else? Don't we long deep in our hearts to be loved in such a way that we are honored and recognized as indispensable, irreplaceable, and unrepeatable? And doesn't it pain our hearts grievously when others treat us merely as objects that can be disposed of and replaced—that is, when others toy with us?

These universal "truths of the heart" were portrayed with remarkable and surprising insight in, of all films, *Toy Story 3* (2010). Little Andy from the previous films isn't so little anymore. In fact, he's headed off to college, and he hasn't played with his toys for years. When the toys steal Andy's cell phone so that their old friend will have to open the toy chest, so they can be seen, you can feel their yearning for love. Andy lifts Rex the dinosaur (voiced again by the "in-con-scchhievable" Wallace Shawn) in order to retrieve his phone, and, once the coast is clear, Rex exclaims with unbridled elation: "He touched me! He touched me!" There it is—the cry of the heart to be loved, to be touched . . . God bless him! Rex was starved for affection. (Listen to me, I think these characters are real people . . . Well, because in a sense they are: they're images of us). I knew then this movie had more to offer than mere entertainment.

New to the series is Lotso the bear, the self-appointed tyrant leader of all the toys at Sunnyside Daycare. In the course of the movie we learn Lotso's tragic backstory. Lotso had been Daisy's most beloved toy. But when she lost him her parents got her another bear *just like him*. When Lotso found out he had been replaced, he "snapped," becoming a "monster inside."

Part of Lotso's revenge for having been cast off and replaced is that if *he* can't be loved, he won't let anybody else be loved either; if he's replaceable, then everybody else is too. At one point Lotso confronts Andy's favorite toy, Woody: "You think you're special, Cowboy? You're a piece of plastic. You were made to be thrown away." When the Ken doll is afraid he's going to lose Barbie, Lotso says: "She's a Barbie doll, Ken. There's a hundred million just like her!" Ken insists: "Not to me there's not"—and Barbie sighs, knowing that Ken loves *her*, knowing that Ken sees her as unrepeatable, irreplaceable.

In the story these toys aren't toys at all. They feel what we feel; they desire what we desire: love. That's why they're so relatable. The theme of *Toy Story 3* is that being replaced and "thrown away" is the opposite of being loved. We all know that in our hearts, but sometimes we're acting out our own "revenge" on others for past hurts, like Lotso. When Lotso seems to be having his way and Woody and his pals are doomed for the incinerator, salvation arrives "from above." In the end, Lotso pays the price for his madness, while love triumphs in the lives of the other toys. Deep stuff for a "kid's movie."

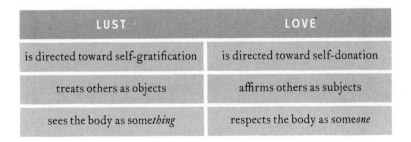

| LUST | LOVE |
|---|---|
| is directed toward self-gratification | is directed toward self-donation |
| treats others as objects | affirms others as subjects |
| sees the body as some*thing* | respects the body as some*one* |

| LUST | LOVE |
| --- | --- |
| sacrifices others for oneself | sacrifices oneself for others |
| grasps at fleeting pleasure | yearns for eternal joy |
| enslaves us | liberates us |
| jealously possesses | confidently trusts |
| manipulates and controls | respects the other's freedom |
| is aimed at any pleasing outlet | is reserved for only one |
| ends when the pleasure ends | lasts through good times and bad |
| makes us feel toyed with | makes us feel treasured |

# CHAPTER 14

# TO INFINITY AND BEYOND

*What I deserve is a man that . . .*
*Delivers me to a destiny, to infinity and beyond*
—BEYONCÉ[1]

Years ago Wendy and I were out to dinner and she observed that something was different about our marriage in recent years, something good. She asked me if I had any insight into what it was. After reflecting a bit I said with a smile, "Yeah, I think I know what it is. I think I've been realizing deep in my heart that you can't satisfy me." She got a big smile on her face and said, "Yeah, *that's* it. And I've been realizing the same thing—you can't satisfy me either." I imagine anyone overhearing us in the restaurant would have thought we were about to get divorced, but to us that realization was cause for joy and celebration. We had never felt closer and freer in our love.

I love my wife more than words can express, and I know she loves me. But I can't possibly be her ultimate satisfaction, and she can't be mine. Sooner or later we must come to terms with the fact that nothing finite can satisfy the "ache" of eros; eros is a yearning for infinity, and we will never be content with anything less. Human love can be, and is designed to be, a beautiful sign or "icon" of infinite fulfillment. But experience attests that if we are expecting another human being to be our ultimate satisfaction, we're placing an unbearable burden on that person, and we've turned the icon into an idol.

Wendy and I knew this in our heads when we got married—that we weren't meant to be each other's ultimate fulfillment—but our hearts were still in some ways "bent" toward each other, expecting and desiring the other to "satisfy the ache." Only slowly, through many painful trials and purifications over the years, have we been learning to release each other from these impossible expectations. It's still a struggle sometimes, but we're learning.

And that's why our conversation at the restaurant was cause for rejoicing. Only to the degree that we stop expecting others to be "god" for us, are we free to love others as they really are, warts and all, without demanding perfection of them, whether a spouse, a friend, a son or daughter, or any other relationship. And only to the degree that we are free from idolizing human love and other human beings are we also free to take our ache for perfect fulfillment to the One who alone can satisfy it. Life begins to make sense, with all its joys and trials. Things take on their proper perspective. And we start to allow our hearts to be dilated, stretched to their maximum capacity—to the point that they are large enough and open enough to receive infinity. Indeed, we become consumed with a burning desire for heaven.

## IMPOVERISHED IMAGES OF HEAVEN

I'd guess you're familiar with Billy Joel's song "Only the Good Die Young." It's a catchy tune, and I almost always find myself moving to the beat when it comes on my car radio. But have you ever listened to the lyrics?

> They say there's a heaven for those who will wait
> Some say it's better but I say it ain't[2]

You know the rest—how he'd rather laugh with the sinners than cry with the saints. Where's that coming from? Probably from the sourpuss "saints" of the starvation-diet gospel. If heaven is an eternal boredom of harps and halos, and the ticket price is saying no to everything I desire here and now, who wants it?

What an impoverished vision of heaven we often have! I just read a letter to the editor in *Time* magazine in which a person laments of heaven: "Sounds pretty dull to me. What do you do with all of that free time? And it goes on forever and ever!"[3] Where do these impoverished impressions of heaven come from? Maybe they come from Saturday morning cartoons (Wile E. Coyote floating on a cloud with wings). Maybe they come from an unshakable sense that doing God's bidding is a hopelessly guilt-ridden, pleasure-less affair. Maybe they come from saccharine-sweet paintings of the heavenly court in which bland drones stand amidst clouds and rainbows wearing those boring standard-issue white robes. If *that's* heaven, the pleasures that advertisers and Hollywood executives parade before us on a daily basis look *far* more attractive.

I would submit that the reason the fast-food gospel looks so attractive is precisely because it presents a convincing counterfeit of what we're really looking for. Indeed, the counterfeit million-dollar bill has the power to deceive us precisely because it looks like the real thing. So I would argue that if we can "untwist" the distortions of the fast-food gospel, we'll be able to rehabilitate and rediscover images of heavenly fulfillment that are actually worth waiting for.

## PLEASURE PRINCIPLES

Unbridled indulgence in sex and alcohol are arguably the two most addictive pleasures offered by the fast-food gospel. There's a reason for that: the joining of man and woman in "one flesh" and the joys of wine are two of the primary biblical images of heaven. We can't forget that Christ's first miracle was at a wedding feast—a celebration of the two becoming "one flesh"—where he enlivens the party with 150 gallons of "the best wine" (see John 2:1–11). Untwist the indulgences of the typical frat party—the abuse of sex and alcohol—and we find ourselves at the wedding feast of Cana, a true foreshadowing of heaven, where rightly directed eros provides "not just fleeting pleasure, but also a certain foretaste of the pinnacle of our existence, of that beatitude [blissful happiness] for which our whole being yearns."[4]

If there's an enemy who wants to keep us from heaven, there's one thing we know about him: he's a plagiarizer. He takes all the good things that belong to God, to Christ and his Church, and puts his name on them, claiming them as his own. If we are to recover more accurate images of heaven, it is imperative that we reclaim what the enemy has plagiarized. Sad thing is, if we tend toward the starvation diet, we may be content to let the enemy have these pleasurable things, seeing nothing really good in them that needs to be reclaimed. Indeed, there are entire camps of "believers" whose basic approach to the pleasurable things of this world (like sex and alcohol) is one of fundamental suspicion.

True enough—things like sex and alcohol are often terribly abused, and whenever good things are abused, pain and despair result. But we mustn't go to the other extreme and blame the good things God has made for our abuse of them. God wants to teach us how to enjoy these gifts and take pleasure in them as he intends. The approach to pleasure, in fact, is one of the distinctive marks of the three "gospels" we've discussed in this book. And each gospel has its own "pleasure principle."

**STARVATION DIET:** Pleasure is an *evil* to reject.

**FAST FOOD:** Pleasure is an *idol* to indulge.

**BANQUET:** Pleasure is an *icon* that's meant to point to heaven.

Or, we could put it this way,

**STARVATION DIET:** If it feels good, it must be sinful.

**FAST FOOD:** If it feels good, do it.

**BANQUET:** If it feels good, it's meant to be a preview of coming attractions.

Or this way,

**STARVATION DIET:** negates the world's pleasures.

**FAST FOOD:** inflates the world's pleasures.

**BANQUET:** sublimates the world's pleasures.

When the world's pleasures are "sublimated" (rightly ordered and lifted up or made "sublime"), then they can be seen for what they are: so many foreshadowings of heavenly bliss. Then we can rejoice wholeheartedly with Saint Brigid of Ireland in her description of heaven as "a great lake of beer"[5] into which we'll dive with holy delight. Then we can get beyond squeamishness and take great joy in the Prophet Isaiah's description of heaven as sucking deeply from the abundant breast of the "New Jerusalem" (an image of the Church as our Mother) and finding comfort in the overflow of her milk (see Isa. 66:11–12). Then we can get beyond prudishness and joyfully recognize the erotic passion of the lovers in the Song of Songs as an image of the divine-human nuptials that await us in heaven (see Eph. 5:31–32; Rev. 19–22).

## EYE HAS NOT SEEN

Heavenly bliss and fulfillment, of course, are beyond all under-standing and description. This means all our earthly images are woefully inadequate. For "no eye has seen, nor ear heard, nor the heart of man conceived, what God has prepared for those who love him" (1 Cor. 2:9). And yet if we are in touch with the "shape" of our infinite yearning, we do gain some dim sense of the fulfillment we hope for. We don't know what it will be, but we know—unless existence is cruel—that fulfillment of our deep-est desires must be possible, even if not in this life. Paraphrasing C. S. Lewis, if I find in myself desires that nothing in this world can satisfy, then it only makes sense that I'm made for another world.[6] Hence, we can describe heaven as a "known unknown."

The term "eternal life," says Benedict XVI, is meant to give a name to this "known unknown." Inevitably, it's an inadequate term that creates confusion, he says. "Eternal" suggests some-thing like the unending succession of days on the calendar. And the term "life" makes us think of our existence here and now. For many, to think of the toil of this life continuing "eternally" seems more like a curse than a gift.[7]

How then are we to understand the term "eternal life"? Benedict XVI insists that it "is not an unending succession of days on the calendar, but something more like the supreme mo-ment of satisfaction in which totality embraces us and we embrace totality." This supreme "moment" of satisfaction, however, is "a moment in which time—the before and after—no longer exists."

It is an infinity of satisfaction that plunges us "into the ocean of infinite love . . . a plunging ever anew into the vastness of being, in which we are simply overwhelmed with joy . . . We must think along these lines," Pope Benedict maintains, "if we want to understand the object of Christian hope, to understand what it is that our faith, our being with Christ, leads us to expect."[8]

## DIVINE NUPTIALS

Let's return to the frame of the biblical narrative: the Bible begins with the earthly marriage of man and woman, and it ends with the heavenly marriage of Christ and the Church. If our ultimate destiny is a fulfillment of eros in "nuptial union" with the divine, and if the nuptials of earth are only a little glimmer of that, it makes complete sense that Christ says we are no longer given in marriage in the life to come (see Matt. 22:30). When eros is fulfilled in Eros, earthly marriage and sexual union will have served their purpose. In other words, you no longer need a sign to point you *to* heaven when you're *in* heaven.

This doesn't mean earthly marriage is simply *deleted*, however. It means earthly marriage will somehow be fulfilled and *completed* in the eternal marriage of Christ and the Church. Christian teaching describes this as a "virginal" reality, but here "virginal" doesn't mean the absence of union; it means the *perfection* of union. It means a union "untouched" by the distortions of sin and lust, a union *completely beyond* the distortions of sin and lust—indeed, beyond anything we have known in this life, and yet somehow not alien to what we have known in this life.[9]

"Virginal" here also refers to the perfect integrity of body and soul. Let us keep in mind that Christianity professes belief not only in some "spiritual" afterlife but also in the *resurrection of the body*. The *Catechism of the Catholic Church* admits: "On no point does the Christian faith encounter more opposition than on the resurrection of the body. It is commonly accepted that the life of the human person continues in a spiritual fashion after death. But how can we believe that this body, so clearly mortal, could rise to eternal life?"[10] Clearly after we die, our bodies return to dust. But is it beyond God to gather that dust once again and "breathe his life into it"? This is the astounding claim of the Christian faith: our bodies will be raised up and "clothed with immortality" (see 1 Cor. 15:54).

And since nothing of our authentic humanity is *deleted*, this means our sexuality also continues in some way in the next life. We will be raised male and female, only this time the divine design for sexuality will be fulfilled in the virginal marriage of Christ and the Church, which includes the everlasting union of all who respond to the wedding invitation of heaven.

## THE COMMUNION OF SAINTS

This eternal consummation in love of all God's sons and daughters is what Christian tradition has called the "communion of saints." "*For man,* this consummation will be the final realization of the unity of the human race, which God willed from creation . . . Those who are united with Christ will form the community of the redeemed, 'the holy city' of God, 'the Bride, the wife of the Lamb.' "[11] The unity that God willed from creation was revealed in our bodies as male and female and the call of the two to spousal union. Somehow, in a mysterious way beyond anything we can think or imagine, all that is masculine in our humanity will be in union with all that is feminine in our humanity, and that one organic union of humanity will be the "one body," the "one virgin Bride" of Christ in union with him forever.

In turn, through that union with Christ, we will be taken up into the ecstasy of the eternal union of Father, Son, and Holy Spirit. Together, in one universal celebration, we will all be intoxicated on God's holy wine, dancing forever in celebration of God's perfect love within the Trinity, God's perfect love for us, our perfect love for him, and our perfect love for one another. It will be a party like we've never known, a universal throwdown lovefest the joys of which we can only dimly imagine.

A student of mine once said, "Sounds like you're describing a drunken orgy or something."

"NO!" I insisted. A drunken orgy is a diabolic mockery of the communion of saints. The devil is not creative. He doesn't have his own "evil world" that runs parallel to God's good world. All he can do is take the good things that God made and twist them, distort them, mock them, plagiarize them. And that's precisely what he's doing in all the perversities that are running unabated in our world today.

We *are* indeed created for a holy kind of inebriation, a nakedness without shame, and a deep intimacy with all of humanity. The enemy takes these truths of God's creation and twists them into some of the grossest distortions the fast-food gospel can dish out. The good news is that Christ came to undo the work of the devil. The more deeply we enter into Christ's death and resurrection, the more we are able to reclaim the glorious truths that have been twisted and distorted by the enemy's lies. Indeed, we must reclaim the pleasures the devil plagiarizes by enduring the painful purification that enables genuine pleasures to blossom in their true, holy expression. If we can do that, we are sure to catch a glimpse of what awaits us in heaven. If not, starvation diet subscribers will view pleasure as the terrain of the *depraved* and fast food subscribers will view heaven as the boring lot of the *deprived*.

Somehow we need to break out of the staid, button-down mold that gives the world the impression that Christians have no fun and heaven is boring. Perhaps that's why I love the hit viral video "JK Wedding Entrance Dance" on YouTube. When the song "Forever" by Chris Brown fills this church, expectations of a normal wedding procession give way to something utterly unexpected—something fresh, free, and loads of fun. The ushers throw their programs in the air, and the wedding party comes two-by-two dancing down the aisle and grooving to the music. And the lyrics are perfect for the occasion:

> It's you and me moving at the speed of light into eternity . . .
> Tonight is the night to join me in the middle of ecstasy[12]

Don't get me wrong: as a Catholic, I'm not lobbying to replace liturgical music with secular dance music. I think it's very important to follow the rubrics of the liturgy as the Church presents them to us (the video was not depicting a Catholic wedding). I'm just saying I love the joy expressed by this wedding party. Each person is so free, so full of life, and each person is expressing his or her own unrepeatable personhood. And—oh!—when the bride comes down the aisle . . . it puts a lump in my throat almost every time I see it.

Think about it: Why do we love weddings so much? Why, for instance, did approximately 2 billion people tune in to the royal wedding of Prince William and Kate Middleton in 2011? Why, especially, do we love to see the bride coming down the aisle? Why do fairy tales so often end with a newly married couple living "happily ever after"? Maybe weddings tap into a deep primordial intuition we have of our destiny, of the ultimate fulfillment of eros in a "fairy-tale wedding" that is no fairy tale at all, but a divine promise of the consummation of the universe, where we really do live "happily ever after."

This is the vision of heaven presented to us in the book of Revelation: a bride coming down the aisle adorned for her husband. It's the vision of "a new heaven and a new earth" in which God wipes away every tear from our eyes, death shall be no more, and neither shall there be mourning, nor crying, nor pain, "for the former things have passed away" and everything is made new (see Rev. 21:1–4).

## THE ULTIMATE FULFILLMENT OF EROS

If this heavenly vision of things is real, then it sure takes a lot of pressure off of sexual love and romance to fulfill us, doesn't it? I'm convinced that the primary reason we get disillusioned in romantic relationships is because we're expecting them to do what only God can do—heal the ache. When we go to the physical and emotional pleasures of sex and romantic love seeking the definitive fulfillment of eros, we have mistaken the shadow for the reality.

I'm reminded of a story I once heard that demonstrates the point. A modern mystic-nun, after giving a presentation in which she shared something of her experiences of "nuptial union" with God, was rebuked by an agnostic psychologist: "You're sick!" he insisted. "What you *really* want is sex. But you're disguising your desire for sex with all this ridiculous talk about union with God." She responded firmly: "Oh no. I beg to differ. What the world *really* wants is union with God, but it's disguising that desire with all this ridiculous sex." Who do you think was right?

If the vision of desire and happiness that we've laid out in this book is real, then maybe those Christians who take up Christ's invitation to forgo marriage "for the sake of the kingdom" (see Matt. 19:12) aren't in fact missing out on the most promising prospect of happiness life has to offer. Maybe instead they're showing the rest of the world where ultimate happiness truly lies: in union with God. Celibacy for the kingdom is not a declaration that sex is "bad." It's a declaration that while sex can be awesome, there's something even better—*infinitely better*! Christian celibacy is a bold declaration that heaven is *real*, and it is worth selling everything to possess.

Of course, we must distinguish between the "wise" and the "unwise" virgins (see Matt. 25:1–13). The unwise "have no oil for their lamps." Their hearts are cold. The fire of eros has been repressed. Father Raniero Cantalamessa observes that if the affections and desires of the heart connected with eros are "systematically denied or repressed" in the name of celibacy, "the result will be double: either one goes on in a tired way, out of a sense of duty, to defend one's image, or more or less licit compensations are sought, to the point of the very painful cases that are afflicting the Church."[13]

The wise virgins, on the other hand, have a full supply of oil, and their lamps (their hearts) are set *on fire*. They do not repress eros. Rather they allow their eros to become what it truly is: a pure, burning, wild, aching longing for God. I'll never forget when the prior of an inner-city monastery pulled me aside after I had given a talk to his community. He pointed out the window to a porn shop across the street and said with a thick French accent: "Zere iz more eros *here* [pointing to the monastery] zen zere iz over zere [pointing to the porn shop]." Then he added, "I'd like to put a sign over zere telling zee people zat what zey are *really* looking for is over here." Amen!

One of the most famous images depicting a "wise virgin" with her lamp on fire is Bernini's marble statue of Teresa of

Avila in ecstasy (see page iv). Here Bernini invites us to contemplate the mystical experience that Teresa herself described
as follows:

> I saw an angel beside me . . . so blazing with light that he
> seemed to be one of the very highest angels, who appear all
> on fire . . . I saw in his hands a long spear of gold, and at the
> end of the iron there seemed to me to be a little fire. This I
> thought he thrust through my heart several times [so deeply]
> that it reached my very entrails. As he withdrew it, I thought it
> brought them with it, and left me all burning with a great love
> of God. So great was the pain, that it made me moan; and so
> utter the sweetness . . . that there was no wanting it to stop, nor
> is there any contenting the soul with less than God.[14]

Teresa speaks of this agonizing ecstasy as something spiritual, "though the body has a share in it," she insists, "indeed, a
great share." It is a "caressing of love so sweet," she says, "that if
anyone thinks I am lying I beseech God, in his goodness, to give
him the same experience." And it *is* an experience that God wants
to share with all of us, in some fashion anyway. While it may be
true that relatively few experience this level of divine ecstasy in
this life, something like this (and far beyond) is destined to be ours
for eternity—if we say "yes" to God's marriage proposal, that is.

Bernini's statue of Teresa in ecstasy is like a stereogram. The
more we enter *in* to it, the more our own lives "pop" in 3D. We

are marked for the stars—for God himself—but in order to reach them, we must give ourselves permission to feel the real depth of our desire (recall that "desire" derives from the Latin phrase *de sidere*: "from the stars"). We must cry out with the psalmist: "My soul yearns and pines for the courts of the Lord. My heart and my flesh cry out for the living God" (Ps. 84:2). "My soul is thirsting for God . . . when can I enter and see his face?" (Ps. 42:3). It's a cry that passes through the prayer of agony but leads to an everlasting prayer of ecstasy.

## WE WILL LIVE AGAIN IN FREEDOM

Perhaps you're one of the sixty million people who has seen the musical *Les Misérables* (which is now a major motion picture). Or perhaps like me you've seen it more times than you can remember. Based on one of the greatest novels ever written and adapted for the stage into one of the most beloved musicals of all time, *Les Misérables* is a profound merging of story and song. Like no other theatrical production I've ever seen it both awakens my yearning for heaven and gives me hope of its fulfillment.

Translated "the poor" or "the miserable ones," *Les Misérables* is a story of the triumph of mercy and love in the face of cold justice and ruthless cruelty. It's a bitter prayer of agony that ends at long last in an eternal prayer of ecstasy. Artfully and poetically, as only story and song can, *Les Misérables* explores the hidden realms of our hearts and beautifully affirms what we long for (*desire*), what we're created for (*design*), and what we're headed for (*destiny*). The final, climactic scene provides a fitting image with which to conclude the reflections of this book.

Jean Valjean is dying after a long and very difficult life. Years earlier he had promised a young mother, Fantine, as she lay dying, that he would raise her daughter, Cosette. Now, on the same day she weds her beloved Marius, Cosette struggles to say good-bye to the man she called her father. When Fantine appears from the life beyond to bid Valjean to join her, the nearness of Valjean's heavenly reward is palpable, and one's heart can't help but swell with joy and anticipation.

As Valjean is reunited with Fantine amidst the chorus of saints in heaven, Marius and Cosette, still dressed for their wedding, stand in the space between heaven and the audience: a bridegroom and his beautiful bride painting an iconic picture for us of the heavenly nuptials that await us in the life to come. Together, the communion of saints in heaven and the communion of man and woman on earth sing of our glorious destiny when, at long last, we will "*live again in freedom | in the garden of the Lord,*" when "*the chain will be broken | and all men will have their reward!*"[15]

Every time I've seen the show there has been a kind of euphoria throughout the theater at this climactic moment, and few dry eyes. What has just happened? Why are people's hearts so deeply moved? They've been given hope: hope that all they yearn for is not in vain; hope that the bitter suffering they've endured in life serves some important, larger purpose; hope that the fairy tale of living happily ever after is not just a fairy tale; hope that there truly is an unending bliss, an unending love, a wedding feast that lasts forever.

> Lord, teach us how to direct our desires according to your design so that we may at long last arrive at so glorious a destiny. Come, Lord, fill these hearts! Amen.

# SCRIPTURES ON DESIRE AND FULFILLMENT

Scripture speaks from beginning to end of human desire and the divine plan to satisfy our hunger. What follows is a collection, largely from the Psalms, of some of my favorite passages on the subject. I find them a source of great consolation and provide them here in the hope that you will too. You might want to read one a day and prayerfully meditate on it.

1. "I will now rain down bread from heaven for you" (Exod. 16:4).

2. "... in the morning you shall have your fill of bread, so that you may know that I, the Lord, am your God" (Exod. 16:12).

3. "This is the bread which the Lord has given you to eat ... everyone had enough to eat" (Exod. 16:15, 18).

4. "I will give you rain in due season, so that the land will bear its crops, and the trees their fruit ... you will have food to eat in abundance" (Lev. 26:4–5).

5. "From there you will seek the Lord your God, and you will find him if you search after him with all your heart and soul" (Deut. 4:29).

6. "He let you be afflicted with hunger, and then fed you with manna, a food unknown to you" (Deut. 8:3).

7. "Will he not bring to fruition . . . my every desire?" (2 Sam. 23:5).

8. " 'Go, eat rich foods and drink sweet drinks . . . for today is holy to our Lord.' . . . Then all the people went to eat and drink . . . and to celebrate with great joy, for they understood the words that had been expounded to them" (Neh. 8:10, 12).

9. "Food from heaven you gave your people in their hunger, water from a rock you sent them in their thirst" (Neh. 9:15).

10. "I myself shall see . . . from my flesh I shall see God; my inmost being is consumed with longing" (Job 19:26–27).

11. "I say to the Lord: 'You are my God. My happiness lies in you alone. He has put into my heart a marvelous love . . .' " (Ps. 16:2–3).

12. "The Lord is my inheritance and my cup; he alone will give me my reward. The measuring line has marked out a lovely place for me; my inheritance is my great delight" (Ps. 16:5–6).

13. "You have made known to me the path of life; you will fill me with joy in your presence, with eternal pleasures at your right hand" (Ps. 16:11).

14. "You have granted him his heart's desire . . . He asked you for life and this you have given" (Ps. 21:2, 4).

15. "The poor shall eat and be satisfied" (Ps. 22:26).

16. "The Lord is my shepherd, there is nothing I shall want" (Ps. 23:1).

17. "You have prepared a banquet for me . . . my cup overflows" (Ps. 23:5).

18. "One thing I ask of the Lord; this I seek; to dwell in the house of the Lord all the days of my life, that I may gaze on the loveliness of the Lord and contemplate his temple" (Ps. 27:4)

19. "Of you my heart has spoken: 'Seek his face' " (Ps. 27:8).

20. "Taste and see that the Lord is good" (Ps. 34:8).

21. "They feast on the riches of your house; they drink from your river of delights" (Ps. 36:8).

22. "Trust in the Lord . . . that you may be fed . . . Delight in the Lord and he will grant you the desires of your heart" (Ps. 37:3–4).

23. "All my longings lie open before you, O Lord; my groans are not hidden from you. My heart throbs" (Ps. 38:9–10).

24. "Like the dear that yearns for running streams, so my soul is yearning for you, my God. My soul is thirsting for God, the God of my life; when can I enter and see the face of God?" (Ps. 42:1–2).

25. "Deep is calling on deep, in the roar of many waters" (Ps. 42:7).

26. "So shall the king greatly desire your beauty" (Ps. 45:11).

27. "O God, you are my God, for you I long; for you my soul is thirsting. My body pines for you like a dry, weary land without water" (Ps. 63:1).

28. "My soul shall be satisfied as with a banquet" (Ps. 63:6).

29. "I am exhausted with calling out, my throat is hoarse, my eyes are worn out with searching for my God" (Ps. 69:3).

30. "Apart from you I want nothing on earth. My body and my heart faint for joy; God is my possession forever" (Ps. 73:25–26).

31. "He split the rocks in the desert. He gave them plentiful drink as from the deep" (Ps. 78:15)

32. "He commanded the clouds above and opened the gates of heaven. He rained down manna for their food and gave them bread from heaven" (Ps. 78:23–24).

33. "They ate and were filled; the Lord gave them what they wanted; they were not deprived of their desire" (Ps. 78:29).

34. "The Lord fed his people with the finest wheat and honey; their hunger was satisfied" (Ps. 81:16).

35. "My soul yearns and pines for the courts of the Lord. My heart and my flesh cry out for the living God" (Ps. 84:2).

36. "They are happy ... in whose hearts are the roads to Zion. As they go through the Bitter Valley they make it a place of springs" (Ps. 84:5–6).

37. "You make springs gush forth in the valleys ... the wild-asses quench their thirst ... earth drinks its fill of your gift" (Ps. 104:10, 11, 13).

38. "He gives us wine to cheer our hearts" (Ps. 104:15).

39. "These all look to you to give them their food at the proper time. When you give it to them ... they are satisfied with good things" (Ps. 104:27–28).

40. "They were hungry and thirsty, and their lives ebbed away. Then they cried out to the Lord in their trouble ... for he satisfies the thirsty and fills the hungry with good things" (Ps. 107:5–6, 9).

41. "Great are the works of the Lord, exquisite in all their delights ... He has given food to those who fear him" (Ps. 111:2, 5).

42. "How sweet to my taste is your promise . . . I gasp with open mouth in my yearning" (Ps. 119).

43. "My soul is waiting for the Lord, I count on his word. My soul is longing for the Lord" (Ps. 130:5–6).

44. "Like a parched land my soul thirsts for you" (Ps. 143:6).

45. ". . . you give them their food at the proper time. You open your hand and satisfy the desires of every living thing" (Ps. 145:15–16).

46. "He fulfills the desire of those who fear him; he hears their cry and saves them" (Ps. 145:19).

47. "It is he who gives bread to the hungry" (Ps. 146:7).

48. "He satisfies you with the finest of wheat" (Ps. 147:14).

49. "Blessed are those who have discovered wisdom . . . nothing you desire can compare with her . . . her ways are filled with delight, her paths all lead to contentment" (Prov. 3:13, 15, 17).

50. "Wisdom . . . has dressed her meat, mixed her wine, yes, she has spread her table. She has sent out her maidens; she calls from the heights out over the city: 'Let whoever is simple turn in here; to him who lacks understanding, I say, Come, eat my food, and drink the wine I have mixed!' " (Prov. 9:1–5).

51. "What the wicked fears overtakes him; what the upright desires comes to him" (Prov. 10:24).

52. "Hope deferred makes the heart sick; desire fulfilled is a tree of life" (Prov. 13:12).

53. "Desire fulfilled is sweet to the soul" (Prov. 13:19).

54. "As an apple tree among the trees of the forest is my beloved . . . With great delight I sat in his shadow, and his fruit was sweet to my taste" (Song 2:3).

55. "He brought me to the banquet hall and his banner over me is love" (Song 2:4).

56. "Let my lover come into his garden and taste its choice fruits. I have come into my garden, my sister, my bride; . . . I have eaten my honeycomb and my honey; I have drunk my wine and my milk. Eat, O friends, and drink; drink your fill, O lovers" (Song 4:16–5:1).

57. "I am my beloved's, his desire is all for me" (Song 7:10).

58. "You nourished your people with . . . bread from heaven, ready to hand, untoiled-for, endowed with all delights and conforming to every taste" (Wis. 16:20).

59. "Come to me, all you who yearn for me, and be filled with my fruits. You will remember me as sweeter than honey, better to have than the honeycomb. He who eats of me will hunger still, he who drinks of me will thirst for more" (Sir. 24:19–21).

60. "I shall wait eagerly for the Lord . . . I shall watch longingly for him" (Isa. 8:17).

61. "My soul yearns for you in the night; in the morning my spirit longs for you" (Isa. 26:9).

62. "He will be gracious to you when you cry out, as soon as he hears he will answer you. The Lord will give you the bread you need and the water for which you thirst" (Isa. 30:19–20).

63. "His food and drink shall be in steady supply" (Isa. 33:16).

64. "The afflicted and the needy seek water in vain, their tongues are parched with thirst. I, the Lord, will answer them . . . I will turn the dry ground into springs of water" (Isa. 41:17–18).

65. "I put water in the desert and rivers in the wasteland for my chosen people to drink" (Isa. 43:20).

66. "I will pour out water upon the thirsty ground and streams upon the dry land" (Isa. 44:3).

67. "With shouts of joy proclaim this, make it known; publish it to the ends of the earth, and say, '. . . They did not thirst when he led them through dry lands; water from the rock he set flowing for them; he cleft the rock and waters welled forth" (Isa. 48:20–21).

68. "All you who are thirsty, come to the water! You who have no money, come receive grain and eat. Come without paying and without cost, drink wine and milk! Why spend your money for what is not bread; your wages for what fails to satisfy? Heed me and you shall eat well, you shall delight in rich fare. Come to me heedfully, listen, that you may have life" (Isa. 55:1–3).

69. "Then you shall be radiant at what you see, your heart shall throb and overflow, for the riches of the sea shall be emptied out before you" (Isa. 60:5).

70. "You will seek me and find me, when you seek me with all your heart" (Jer. 29:13).

71. "And then, on that day, the mountains shall drip new wine, and the hills shall flow with milk. And the channels of Judah shall flow with water: A fountain shall issue from the house of the Lord" (Joel 3:18).

72. "Jesus said: 'My heart is moved with pity for the crowd, for they have been with me now for three days and have nothing to eat. I do not want to send them away hungry, for fear they may collapse on the way.' . . . They all ate and were satisfied" (Matt. 15:32, 37).

73. "The kingdom of heaven may be likened to a king who gave a wedding feast for his son . . . 'Behold, I have prepared my banquet . . . and everything is ready; come to the feast'" (Matt. 22:1–4).

74. "The wedding feast is ready . . . Go out, therefore, into the main roads, and invite everyone . . . The servants went out into the streets and gathered all they found, both bad and good alike, and the hall was filled with guests" (Matt. 22:8–10).

75. "He has filled the hungry with good things" (Luke 1:53).

76. "You will eat and drink at my table in my kingdom" (Luke 22:30).

77. "Jesus answered the [thirsty woman], 'If you knew the gift of God . . . you would have asked him and he would have given you living water . . . Everyone who drinks this water will be thirsty again, but whoever drinks the water I give him will never thirst'" (John 4:10, 13–14).

78. "Jesus then took the loaves, gave thanks, and distributed them . . . so also the fish, as much as they wanted . . . the loaves had been more than they could eat" (John 6:11, 13).

79. "Amen, amen, I say to you, you are looking for me . . . because you ate the loaves and were filled. Do not work for food that perishes but for food that endures for eternal life, which the Son of Man will give you" (John 6:26–27).

80. "I am the bread of life; whoever comes to me will never hunger, and whoever believes in me will never thirst" (John 6:35).

81. "I am the living bread that came down from heaven; whoever eats this bread will live forever; and the bread that I will give is my flesh for the life of the world" (John 6:51).

82. "On the last and greatest day of the Feast, Jesus stood and said in a loud voice, 'If anyone is thirsty, let him come to me and drink . . . He who believes in me, as the Scripture has said, 'streams of living water will flow from within him' " (John 7:37–38).

83. "He has shown kindness by giving you rain from heaven and . . . he provides you with plenty of food and fills your hearts with joy" (Acts 14:17)

84. "I have learned the secret of being well fed and of going hungry, of living in abundance and of being in need . . . God will fully supply whatever you need, in accord with his glorious riches" (Phil. 4:12, 19).

85. "They will not hunger or thirst anymore . . . For the Lamb [Christ] . . . will lead them to springs of life-giving water, and God will wipe away every tear from their eyes" (Rev. 7:16–17).

86. "To him who is thirsty I will give to drink without cost from the spring of the water of life" (Rev. 21:6).

*The Virtue of Chastity*, St. Peter's Basilica; Rome, Italy
(©2008 MARK A. NORTHROP, OFWC MEDIA, LLC)

# NOTES

## WHAT THIS BOOK IS ABOUT

1. *Letter to Artists* (April 4, 1999) 10.

## CHAPTER 1: THE UNIVERSAL LONGING

1. Bruce Springsteen, "Hungry Heart," from the album *The River* (Columbia Records, 1980).

2. From the documentary film *The Heart Is a Drum Machine*, directed by Pomerenke (2009).

3. http://rockhall.com/inductees/u2/transcript/bruce-springsteen-on-u2/.

4. John Paul II, *Man and Woman He Created Them: A Theology of the Body* (Pauline, 2006), 47:2. Henceforth this work will be cited with the abbreviation *TOB*.

5. *Magnificat*, December 2001, pp. 2–3.

6. Catholic author and philosophy professor Peter Kreeft observes that biblical authors "did not divide reality into two mutually exclusive categories of purely immaterial spirit and purely nonspiritual matter. Rather, they saw all matter as in-formed, in-breathed by spirit." And this vision, he says, applied especially to "the human body, nature's masterpiece and microcosm." In the modern world, on the other hand, René Descartes "initiates 'angelism' when he says, 'My whole essence is in thought alone' ['I think therefore I am']. Matter and spirit now become 'two clear and distinct ideas.' . . . This is *our* common sense; we have inherited these categories, like nonremovable contact lenses, from Descartes, and it is impossible for us to understand pre-Cartesian thinkers while we wear them. Thus we are constantly reading our modern categories anachronistically into the authors of the Bible" (*Everything You Ever Wanted to Know about Heaven—But Never Dreamed of Asking* [Ignatius Press, 1990], pp. 86–87).

7. Sexuality "is by no means something purely biological, but concerns the innermost being of the human person as such" (John Paul II, *On the Christian Family in the Modern World* [November 22, 1981] 11).

8. *TOB*, 7:2

9. Pope Benedict XVI, *God Is Love* (December 25, 2005) 11.

10. Ibid., 4.

11. Lorenzo Albacete, *God at the Ritz: Attraction to Infinity* (Crossroads, 2002), p. 120.

## CHAPTER 2: THE STARVATION DIET

1. R.E.M., "Losing My Religion," from the album *Out of Time* (Warner Bros., 1991).

2. John Eldredge, *The Journey of Desire: Searching for the Life We Only Dreamed Of* (Thomas Nelson, 2000), p. 41.

3. Ibid., p. 30.

4. "Madonna's Next Chapter," *Ladies Home Journal*, July 2005, p. 126.

5. "The first Protestant reformers . . . taught that original sin has radically perverted man and destroyed his freedom." In this view, "the tendency to evil . . . would be insurmountable." Catholic teaching is that original sin caused "a deprivation of original holiness and justice, but human nature has not been totally corrupted: it is wounded . . . and inclined to sin—an inclination to evil that is called 'concupiscence.' Baptism, by imparting the life of Christ's grace, erases original sin and turns a man back toward God, but the consequences for nature, weakened and inclined to evil, persist in man and summon him to spiritual battle" (*Catechism of the Catholic Church* 406, 405; hereafter abbreviated as *CCC*).

6. Pope Benedict XVI, *Light of the World: The Pope, the Church and the Signs of the Times* (Ignatius Press, 2010), p. 103.

## CHAPTER 3: FAST FOOD

1. Peter Gabriel, "Blood of Eden," from the album *Us* (Virgin Records, 1992).

2. Saint Augustine, Homily on First Letter of John. *Homilies on the First Letter of John*, Ramsey Boniface, trans., *Works of Saint Augustine, A Translation for the 21st Century* (New City Press, 2008).

3. "Companies Buy into Quirky Film Idea," *Lancaster (PA) Sunday News*, February 6, 2011, p. D1.

4. James K. A. Smith, *Desiring the Kingdom: Worship, Worldview, and Cultural Formation* (Baker Academic, 2009), pp. 75–76.

5. Saint Augustine, Homily on First Letter of John.

6. Sigmund Freud, "On the Universal Tendency to Debasement in the Sphere of Love," sct. 3.

7. C. S. Lewis, *The Weight of Glory* (HarperCollins, 2001), p. 26.

8. Pope Benedict XVI, *God Is Love* 7.

9. Countless websites attribute this quote to Woody Allen, but finding the original source has alluded me.

10. dailybruin.com/news/ 2003/jan/15/sexual-aging/.

## CHAPTER 4: THE BANQUET

1. Steve Winwood, "Higher Love," from the album *Back in the High Life* (Island Records, 1986).

2. In the context of discussing physical hunger and our desire for heaven, I like G. K. Chesterton's observation: "Even what we call our material desires are spiritual, because they are human . . . [S]cience cannot analyze any man's wish for a pork chop, and say how much of it is hunger, how much custom, how much nervous fancy, how much a haunting love of the beautiful. The man's desire for the pork chop remains literally as mystical . . . as his desire for heaven" (*Heretics* [Arc Manor, 2006], p. 75).

3. Pope John Paul II, *Faith and Reason* (September 14, 1998) 12.

4. *CCC*, 2014.

5. *CCC*, 125, 139.

6. Pope Benedict XVI, *God Is Love* 10.

7. *CCC*, 27.

8. Saint Augustine, Homily on First Letter of John.

9. *CCC*, 30.

10. Pope John Paul II, *The Redeemer of Man* (March 4, 1979) 18.

11. Albacete, *God at the Ritz: Attraction to Infinity*, p. 154.

12. Communion Antiphon, Sunday Liturgy, January 16, 2011.

13. Order of the Mass.

14. "Wine cellar" is Teresa's preferred translation for what is often rendered the King's "chambers" in Song of Songs 1:4.

15. Cited in Blaise Arminjon, *The Cantata of Love: A Verse by Verse Reading of the Song of Songs* (Ignatius Press, 1988), p. 71.

16. Pope Benedict XVI, *God Is Love* 7.

17. Ibid., 9.

18. Father Raniero Cantalamessa, "The Two Faces of Love: Eros and Agape," First Lenten Sermon to the Roman Curia, March 25, 2011; www.zenit.org/article-32122?/=english.

19. Pope Benedict XVI, *God Is Love* 9.

20. Pope Benedict XVI, General Audience, November 26, 2008.

21. Eldredge, *Journey of Desire*, pp. 46–47.

22. A great many Internet cites attribute this saying to Saint Augustine, but I am unable to find the original source.

23. Saint Bonaventure, *The Soul's Journey into God* (Paulist Press, 1978), p. 55.

24. Father Simon Tugwell, *The Beatitudes: Soundings in Christian Traditions* (Templegate Publishers, 1980), p. 78.

25. G. K. Chesterton, *Orthodoxy* (Ignatius Press, 1995), p. 102.

26. Steppenwolf, "Born to Be Wild," written by Mars Boniface, from the album *Steppenwolf* (ABC Dunhill, 1968).

27. Tugwell, *The Beatitudes*, p. 78.

28. This untitled hymn appeared in *Magnificat*, December 14, 2010.

## CHAPTER 5: THE LIVING HOPE OF SATISFACTION

1. U2, "I Still Haven't Found What I'm Looking For," from the album *The Joshua Tree* (Island Records, 1987).

2. Steve Stockman, *Walk On: The Spiritual Journey of U2* (Relevant Books, 2001), p. 72.

3. *TOB*, 112:4.

4. Caryll Houselander, *The Reed of God* (Ave Maria Press, 2006), p. 121.

5. Saint Thérèse of Lisieux, *Story of a Soul* (ICS Publications, 1976), pp. 192, 193, 196, 197, 181, 276, 101.

6. Houselander, *The Reed of God*, pp. 134–35.

7. *CCC*, 1817.

8. *CCC*, 1818.

9. Pope Benedict XVI, *Saved in Hope* (November 30, 2007) 1.

10. Saint Augustine, *On the Trinity* XIII 5:8.

11. Pope John Paul II, *Lord and Giver of Life* (May 18, 1986) 51.

## CHAPTER 6: EXPOSING AND STRETCHING OUR HEARTS

1. Johnny Cash, "Ring of Fire," from the album *Ring of Fire: The Best of Johnny Cash* (Columbia Records, 1963).

2. Karol Wojtyla, *Love and Responsibility* (Ignatius Press, 1981), p. 46.

3. Jacques Philippe, *Interior Freedom* (Scepter Publishers, 2007), p. 113.

4. Joseph Cardinal Ratzinger, *Mary: The Church at the Source*, trans. Adrian Walker (Ignatius Press, 2005), p. 15 (emphasis added).

5. Saint Augustine, *Enarrationes in Psalmos* 37.14.

6. Saint Teresa of Avila, *The Book of Her Life*, in *The Collected Works of St. Teresa of Avila*, vol. 1 (ICS Publications, 1976), p. 319.

7. *CCC*, 2711.

8. Ibid.

9. "The man who prays," wrote Cardinal Ratzinger, "tries to approach the Lord and thus seeks to enter into nuptial union with him" (*The Spirit of the Liturgy* [Ignatius Press, 2000], p. 197).

10. *TOB*, 12:5, n.22.

11. Pope John Paul II, *At the Dawn of the New Millennium* (January 6, 2001) 33.

12. Philippe, *Interior Freedom*, pp. 125–26.

13. Pope Benedict XVI, *Saved in Hope* 33.

14. Saint Augustine, Homily on First Letter of John.

15. *CCC*, 2544, 2556.

16. Saint Teresa of Avila, *Life*, p. 123.

17. *Catherine of Siena: The Dialogue*, trans. Suzanne Noffke, O.P., *The Classics of Western Spirituality* (Paulist Press, 1980), chapter 54, p. 107.

18. *TOB*, 48:1.

19. Saint Teresa of Avila, *The Interior Castle*, in *The Collected Works of St. Teresa of Avila*, vol. 2 (ICS Publications, 1980), p. 378.

20. Tugwell, *The Beatitudes*, p. 81.

## CHAPTER 7: OUR BODIES TELL THE STORY

1. John Mayer, "Your Body Is a Wonderland," from the album *Room for Squares* (Columbia Records, 2002).

2. Marc Grossman, *Magic Eye Beyond 3D: Improve Your Vision* (Andrews McMeel Publishing, 2004).

3. John Paul Young, "Love Is in the Air," written by George Young and Harry Vanda, from the album *Love Is in the Air* (Albert Productions, 1977).

4. Caryll Houselander, *The Mother of Christ* (Sheed and Ward, 1978), p. 34.

5. "The Sound of Music," from the original sound track recording from the 1965 film, *The Sound of Music*, composed by Richard Rogers, lyrics by Oscar Hammerstein (RCA Victor, 1965).

6. What follows in this paragraph is adapted from Peter Kreeft's reflections in *Everything You Ever Wanted to Know About Heaven*, p. 125.

7. Ibid.

8. *TOB*, 101:4; 102:8.

9. *TOB*, 87:6.

10. The "great mystery" revealed in the linking of the one-flesh union with the union of Christ and the Church, John Paul II tells us, "*signifies the mystery* first hidden in God's mind and later revealed in man's history. Given its importance, the mystery is '*great*' *indeed*." For it reveals "God's salvific plan for humanity," and, as such, "that mystery is in some sense the central theme of the whole of revelation, its central reality. It is what God as Creator and Father wishes above all to transmit to mankind in his Word" (*TOB*, 93:2). In this way, as John Paul II wrote elsewhere, "Saint Paul's magnificent synthesis concerning the 'great mystery' appears as the compendium or *summa*, in some sense, *of the teaching about God and man* which was brought to fulfillment by Christ" (*Letter to Families* [February 2, 1994] 19).

11. Saint Bonaventure, *Bringing Forth Christ: Five Feasts of the Child Jesus*, trans. Eric Doyle (Fairacres, 1984).

12. Peter Kreeft, *Heaven, the Heart's Deepest Longing* (Ignatius Press, 1980), p. 35.

13. Ratzinger, *Spirit of the Liturgy*, p. 96.

14. Ratzinger, *Mary: The Church at the Source*, p. 15.

15. Ibid., pp. 88–89.

16. Ratzinger, *Spirit of the Liturgy*, p. 142.

17. Saint Augustine, *Sermo Suppositus* 120.

18. Pope John Paul II, *On the Dignity and Vocation of Women* (August 15, 1988) 26.

19. *TOB*, 19:4.

20. Peter Gabriel, "In Your Eyes," from the album *So* (Real World Records, 1986).

## CHAPTER 8: IN THE BEGINNING

1. "Sigh No More" from the album *Sigh No More* (Island Records, 2009).

2. He credits Robert A. Burton's book *On Being Certain* (St. Martin's Press, 2009) as the source of this exercise.

3. Albacete, *God at the Ritz*, p. 154.

4. *TOB*, 46:5; 55:4.

5. *TOB*, 43:7.

6. *CCC*, 375.

7. *TOB*, 34:1, note 47.

8. Reported in Laura Sessions Stepp's book *Unhooked: How Young Women Pursue Sex, Delay Love and Lose at Both* (Riverhead Books, 2007), p. 29.

9. Saint Augustine, *Sermon* 69, c. 2, 3.

10. *TOB*, 29:4.

## CHAPTER 9: TRUSTING GOD'S DESIGNS

1. Mike Mangione, "The Killing Floor," from the album *Tenebrae* (Dualtone/Rodzinka Records, 2008).

2. *The Devil's Advocate* was based on a novel by Andrew Neiderman, was directed by Taylor Hickford, and released in 1997 by Warner Brothers, New Regency Pictures.

3. *CCC*, 396.

4. *CCC*, 397.

5. Saint Louis de Montfort, *True Devotion to the Blessed Virgin* 45.

6. *Magnificat*, Holy Week, 2010, p. 124.

7. Tom Petty, "The Waiting," from the album *Hard Promises* (Backstreet, 1981).

8. Pope John Paul II, *Lord and Giver of Life* 51.

9. Pope John Paul II, *Crossing the Threshold of Hope* (Knopf, 1994), p. 228.

10. This rejection of our "receptive" posture can also be described as a rejection of our "bridal" posture before God. We don't want to be the "bride," we want to be our own "masculine" lords. And this, as I once heard it said, places us in a "quasi-homosexual" relationship with God since, because of our rebellious posture, there are now two "masculine" principles, two bridegrooms. And when there are two bridegrooms, there's no possibility of a "holy communion" between them, and there's no possibility of generating new life. Truly, our bodies tell the story, and we must learn to listen to what they are "saying" to us. For when we fail to live the sexual difference rightly as a call to holy communion, this failure also obscures our call to Holy Communion with God.

11. *CCC*, 398.

12. "The Killing Floor," from the album *Tenebrae* (Dualtone/Rodzinka Records, 2008).

## CHAPTER 10: THE DESIGNS OF REDEMPTION

1. Switchfoot, "Dare You to Move," from the album *Beautiful Letdown* (Columbia Records, 2003).

2. Pope John Paul II, *Crossing the Threshold of Hope*, p. 66.

3. *CCC*, 657.

## CHAPTER 11: CHASTITY IS A PROMISE OF IMMORTALITY

1. Bangles, "Eternal Flame," composed by Susanna Hoffs, Tom Kelly, and Billy Steinberg, from the album *Everything* (Columbia Records, 1988).

2. *CCC*, 1024, 1035.

3. *CCC*, 2347.

4. For a discussion about the specifics of the most frequently asked questions of sexual morality, see my book *Good News About Sex and Marriage: Answers to Your Honest Questions About Catholic Teaching* (Servant, 2000, 2006).

5. The word "unicorn" appears nine times in the King James Version of the Old Testament (see Num. 23:22, 24:8; Deut. 33:17; Job 39:9, 39:10; Ps. 22:21; Ps. 29:6; Ps. 92:10; Isa. 34:7). It comes from the Hebrew word *reym* or *re'em*. The Greek is *monokeros*, which means "one-horned." It is often rendered "wild ox."

6. Chris Lavers, *The Natural History of Unicorns* (William Morrow, 2009), cover flap.

7. Wojtyla, *Love and Responsibility*, pp. 169, 170.

8. *CCC*, 2337.

9. *CCC*, 2339.

10. *TOB*, 43:6.

## CHAPTER 12: FREEING FREEDOM

1. U2, "Miracle Drug," from the album *How to Dismantle an Atomic Bomb* (Interscope Records, 2004).

2. Albacete, *God at the Ritz: Attraction to Infinity*, p. 113.

3. *TOB*, 126:5.

4. Pope John Paul II, *The Splendor of the Truth* (August 6, 1993) 18.

5. *CCC*, 1968.

## CHAPTER 13: LOVING LOVE

1. The Shirelles, "Will You Still Love Me Tomorrow," written by Gerry Goffin and Carole King, from the album *Tonight's the Night* (Scepter Records, 1961).

2. Pope Benedict XVI, *God Is Love* 5.

3. Ibid., 4.

4. Cantalamessa, "The Two Faces of Love."

5. Pope John Paul II, general audience of March 5, 1997.

6. Saint Thérèse of Lisieux, *Story of a Soul*, p. 103.

7. See Wojtyla, *Love and Responsibility*, pp. 150–51.

8. Ibid., p. 139.

9. Ibid., p. 146.

10. Ibid., p. 83.

11. Ibid., pp. 83–84.

12. Ibid., p. 135.

13. Ibid., pp. 87–88.

14. Rocco Buttiglione, *Karol Wojtyla: The Thought of the Man Who Became John Paul II* (Eerdman's, 1997), p. 100.

15. Ibid., p. 102.

## CHAPTER 14: TO INFINITY AND BEYOND

1. Beyoncé, "Single Ladies," from the album *I Am . . . Sasha Fierce* (Columbia Records, 2008).

2. Billy Joel, "Only the Good Die Young," from the album *The Stranger* (Columbia Records, 1977).

3. *Time*, April 30, 2012, p. 8.

4. Pope Benedict XVI, *God Is Love* 4.

5. Augusta Gregory, *A Book of Saints and Wonders*, Book I: *St. Brigit, the Mary of the Gael* (Web, PDF), p. 6., http://www.mythicalireland.com/mythology/tuathade/brigit.html.

6. C. S. Lewis, *Mere Christianity* (HarperSanFrancisco, 2001), pp. 136–37.

7. Pope Benedict XVI, *Saved in Hope* 10, 12.

8. Ibid., 12.

9. *TOB*, 69:5

10. *CCC*, 996.

11. *CCC*, 1045; italics in original.

12. Chris Brown, "Forever," from the album *Exclusive: The Forever Edition* (Jive, Zomba, 2008).

13. Cantalamessa, "The Two Faces of Love."

14. *The Life of Teresa of Jesus*, section xxix, 16–17.

15. "Do You Hear the People Sing" (reprise/finale), *Les Misérables*, music by Claude-Michel Shonberg, English libretto by Herbert Kretzmer.

## ACKNOWLEDGMENTS

My deep gratitude goes to the following men and women who helped with this book: Gary Jansen and all the production team at Random House, Karen Goodwin, Claudia Cross, Jason Clark, Mark Wassmer, David Kang, Mike Mangione, Mary Kate McNulty, David Leiberg, Nancy LeSourd, David Abel, Nathan West, Michael Field, Tony Verheyen, and Dawn Woodsen.

## ABOUT THE AUTHOR

Christopher West is a renowned educator, bestselling author, cultural commentator, and popular theologian who specializes in making the dense scholarship of the late Pope John Paul II's *Theology of the Body* accessible to a wide audience. As founder of The Cor Project, he leads a nonprofit global outreach devoted to cultural renewal through the "new evangelization." His extensive lecturing, his numerous books and articles, his popular audio and video programs, and his multiple media appearances—millions have seen him on Fox News, ABC News, MSNBC, and EWTN—have sparked an international groundswell of interest in the late pope's teaching across denominational lines.

West has been teaching graduate and undergraduate courses on the *Theology of the Body* and sexual ethics since the late 1990s, having served on the faculty of St. John Vianney Theological Seminary in Denver and the Institute for Priestly Formation at Creighton University in Omaha and as a visiting professor at the John Paul II Institute in Melbourne, Australia. Since 2004 he has served as a research fellow and faculty member of the Theology of the Body Institute near Philadelphia. His courses there continue to draw clergy, religious, and lay people from around the globe. He also serves as a visiting faculty member of the Saint Therese Institute of Faith and Mission in Bruno, Saskatchewan, Canada.

Of all his titles and accomplishments, Christopher is most proud to call himself a devoted husband and father. He lives near Lancaster, Pennsylvania, with his wife, Wendy, and their five children.

Stay connected with Christopher West:
Visit christopherwest.com and click "subscribe."
Like "Christopher West (Official)" on Facebook.
For dates, information, and tickets on the
*Fill These Hearts* tour: visit fillthesehearts.org.

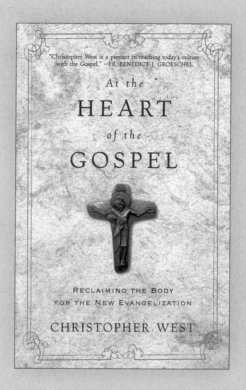